This book is dedicated to
all the youth in Summit County
who dare to create.

Be Brave.

Be Bold.

Imagine the possibilities.

Impact the world around you.

Copyright © 2018 by Summit County Youth
and Breckenridge Creative Arts

All rights reserved.

Breckenridge Creative Arts

150 West Adams Avenue

Post Office Box 4269

Breckenridge, CO 80424

info@breckcreate.org

ISBN-13:

978-1987735895

ISBN-10:

1987735897

Contents

Forward...05
Intro..07
Yarn: Lindsay Eland................................08
Acknowledgments.................................105
About Breckenridge Creative Arts.........106
About The After School Writing Club....108

Short Stories

Scaredy Cat: Hannah Silva.....................12
The Coming: Juniper Lee........................16
If I Could Change A Day: Jadyn Dalrymple............23
Spotlight: Anna Vos................................26
394 Starlet Lane: Maggie Butler.............30
Life and Death of _____: Jack Crowe...............36
Ocean Vacation: Bella Butler.................41
Learning to Ride: Cami Davis.................49
July 29: Juniper Lee................................52
Crash: Nascha Martinez..........................60
Hunted by Swords: Peri Habermas........66
Saving The Titanic: Mary Grace Butler....72
Oh, What Would I Do Without You?:
Anya Waldes...78
The Dreams: Mandy Clawson.................83
Spy: Ella Meltzer......................................91
Hard Work: Cole Stuckey........................99
Growth and Strength: Luci Brady..........102

Poetry

Labels: Ella Eland....................................25
So Much More: Ella Eland.......................25
Blah Blah Blah: Ella Eland......................47
Quiet: Ella Eland......................................47
Amor: Aida Guerra...................................58
Portrait of Nana: Cooper McMullen........67
Nature in Winter: Luke Klasnick.............73

Artwork

Artist: Ella Eland....................................cover
Spider: Elliott Foster...............................03
Bento Box: Estrella Guadamuz..............04
Kool Koala: Natalie Leyva.......................06
Junk Food Chimney: Annika Fowles......09
The Gift of a View: Matthew Shaffer......10
Elephant: Issac Dalrymple.....................13
Skiing: Zach Nelson................................14
Koi Fish: Annika Fowles..........................19
Expressive Eyes Gorilla: Logan Pappas...20
Inuit Child: Littlepage Green..................22
Tree: Luke Klasnick.................................24
Kaleidoscope Vision: Ella Eland............27
Lakes and Snowmobiles: Matthew Shuttleworth.29
Falling: Emily Sandberg..........................33
Expressive Eyes and Meaningful Tattoos:
Rex Andrews...34
Expressive Pen Drawing: Cyle Goff.......37
Through The Eyes: Allison Moreno Ramirez...........38
Untitled Masterpiece: Jacqueline Rodriguez........40
Imagine Warm-up: Benjamin Dyke........43
Izzy: Grace Butler...................................44
Solar System: Guadalupe Barrientos....46
Husky: Paola Arrieta...............................48
Expressive Eyes Mountain Goat:
Elizabeth Smith......................................50
Abstract Rhythm and Pattern: Haley Davis...........55
Zentangle Seascape: Hunter Stimson...56
World Split in Two: Julia Horvath..........59
Mermaid: Victor Dominguez...................63
Shattered Value Cityscape: Bridgette Hough.......64
Shattered Value Carnations: Soledad Borrego......68
Ranch Horse: Miguel Gomez..................70
Expressive Eyes: Amber Walsh.............75
Aspen Forest Zentangles: Mackenna Simson.......76
Imagine Feeling Loved: Natalie Leyva...79

Teton Barn: Oliver Trowbridge	80
Bowie: Gwen Goodenbour	82
Wheelin' Around the World: Johnny Lunney	86
Peregrine Falcon: Issac Dalrymple	88
Self-Portrait: Britney Venegas	90
Instagram Eyes: Haley Davis	95
African Fox: Raina Miller	96
Untitled: Chase Byers	98
Still Life: Kiara Gelbman	100
Sushi Delight: Abraham Lopez	103
Untitled: Jennifer Amador	104
Woof!: Ruby Gerard	107
Dragon: William O'Brien	108
Leopard: Christopher Lopez	110
Untitled: Jacqueline Jasso	back cover

Cover Image:
Artist
Colored pencils on Artagain Paper
Ella Eland, Grade 8

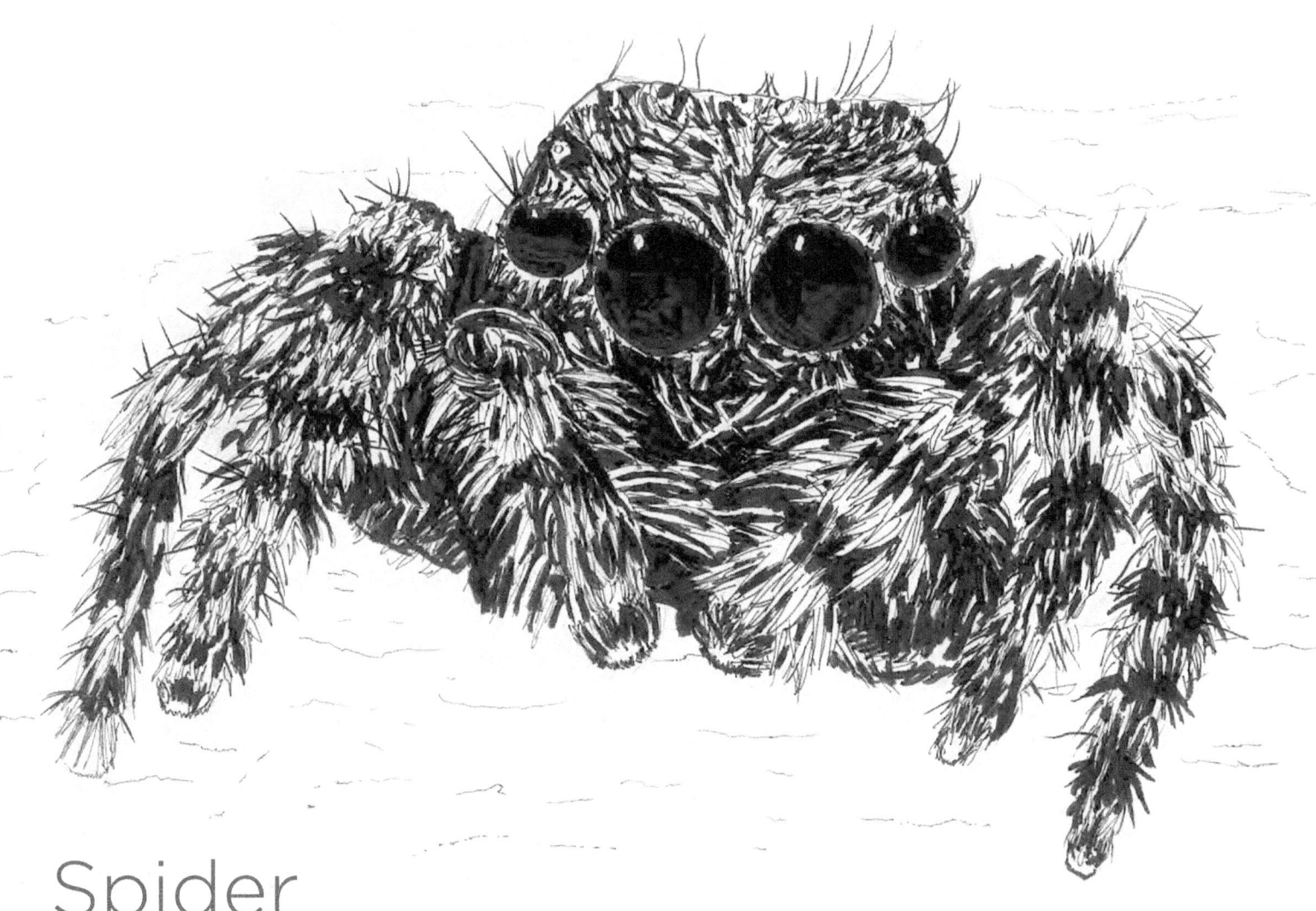

Spider
Ink | Elliott Foster, Grade 9

I am 15 years old, born and raised in Summit County. As a Summit High School Freshman, I believe drawing is a healthy break from work and school. Throughout my education, I have found myself able to apply my creativity to writing, and additionally, to sports such as snowmobiling and dirt biking and baseball.

Bento Box

Ceramic | Estrella Guadamuz, Grade 6

I am 11 and currently in 6th grade. In my family, my dad was born in Costa Rica, but my mom was born in Minnesota. Also, my mom's best friend has lived with us since I can remember. My sister and I have lived in Summit our whole lives. I have always loved art but not as much as I have started to this year. I honestly prefer 2D Art more than 3D because I believe I am better at it and enjoy it more.

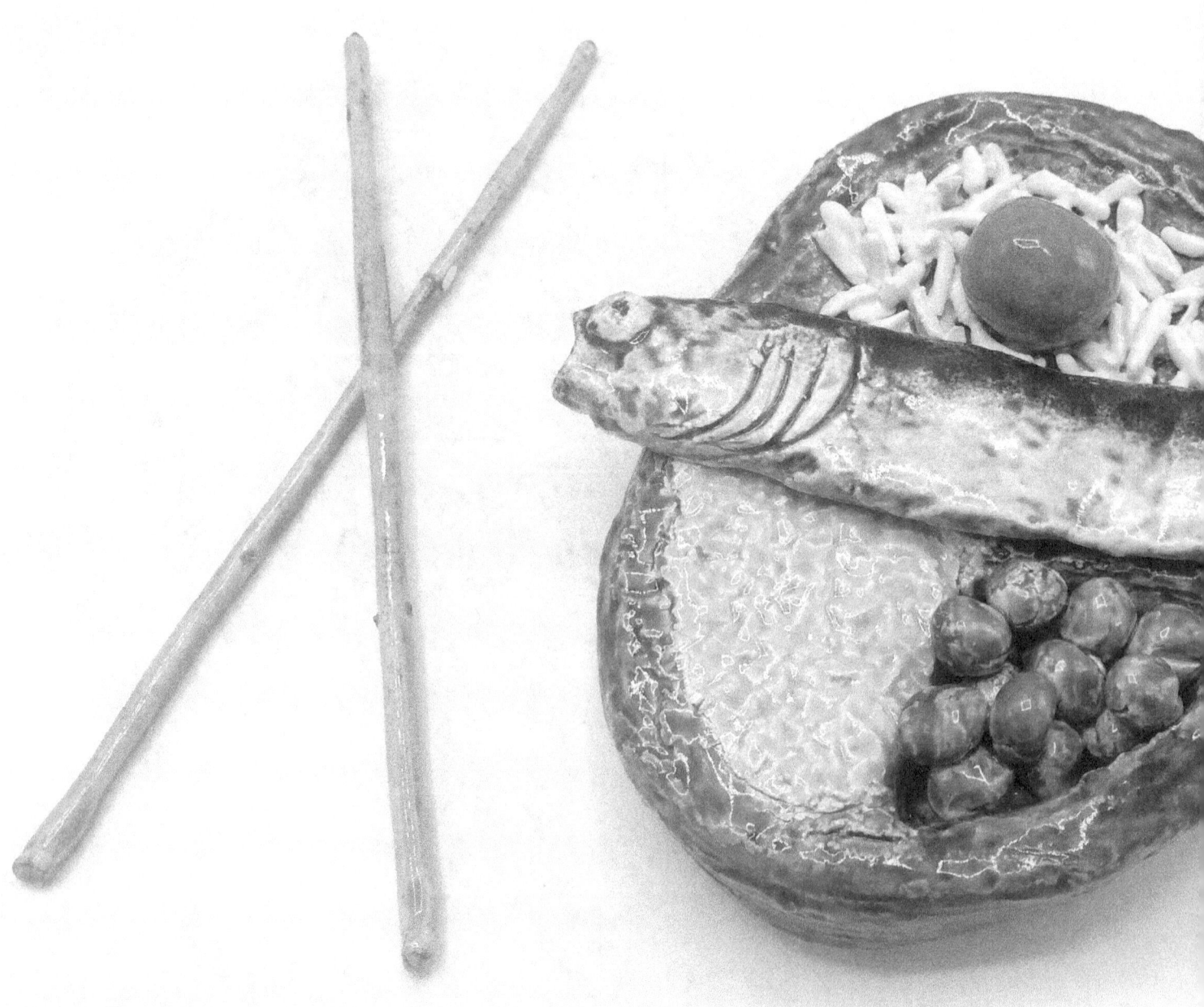

Forward

How exactly does a book come into being? This particular one began by imagining. We wondered, "What if?"

What if young authors and artists had an opportunity to share their creativity with their families, community, and the world? What if they could see how their ideas made an impact on those around them and not just on their report card? What if they inspired each other to do more, create more, be more?

That was our hope for this book. We wanted to launch young creatives into a lifetime of art and writing.

This is the first collection of creative writing and artwork from Middle School and High School age students in Summit County, CO. Joining forces with BreckCreate, local authors and artists, teachers, and parents, we kept our eyes open for those talented minds and nudged them to have courage and put "pencil to paper" and share their craft with our community.

We hope you enjoy this collection, and along with these students, that you imagine. Be inspired, and imagine your own possibilities.

Sonya Dalrymple
After-School Writing Club Instructor, Breckenridge Creative Arts

Karen S. Fischer
Teen Art Club Instructor, Breckenridge Creative Arts
Visual Arts Teacher, Summit High School

Kool Koala

Colored Pencil
Natalie Leyva, Grade 11

My name is Natalie Leyva. I am attending school at Summit High School and currently a junior. I was born in Vail, Colorado and grew up in Summit County my whole life being surrounded by mountains and beautiful scenery. I have always loved art and the way I can just focus on that and nothing else. It's my distraction from my everyday life. My medium is a koala that represented a lot of patterns. It was about being expressive and showing my favorite animal.

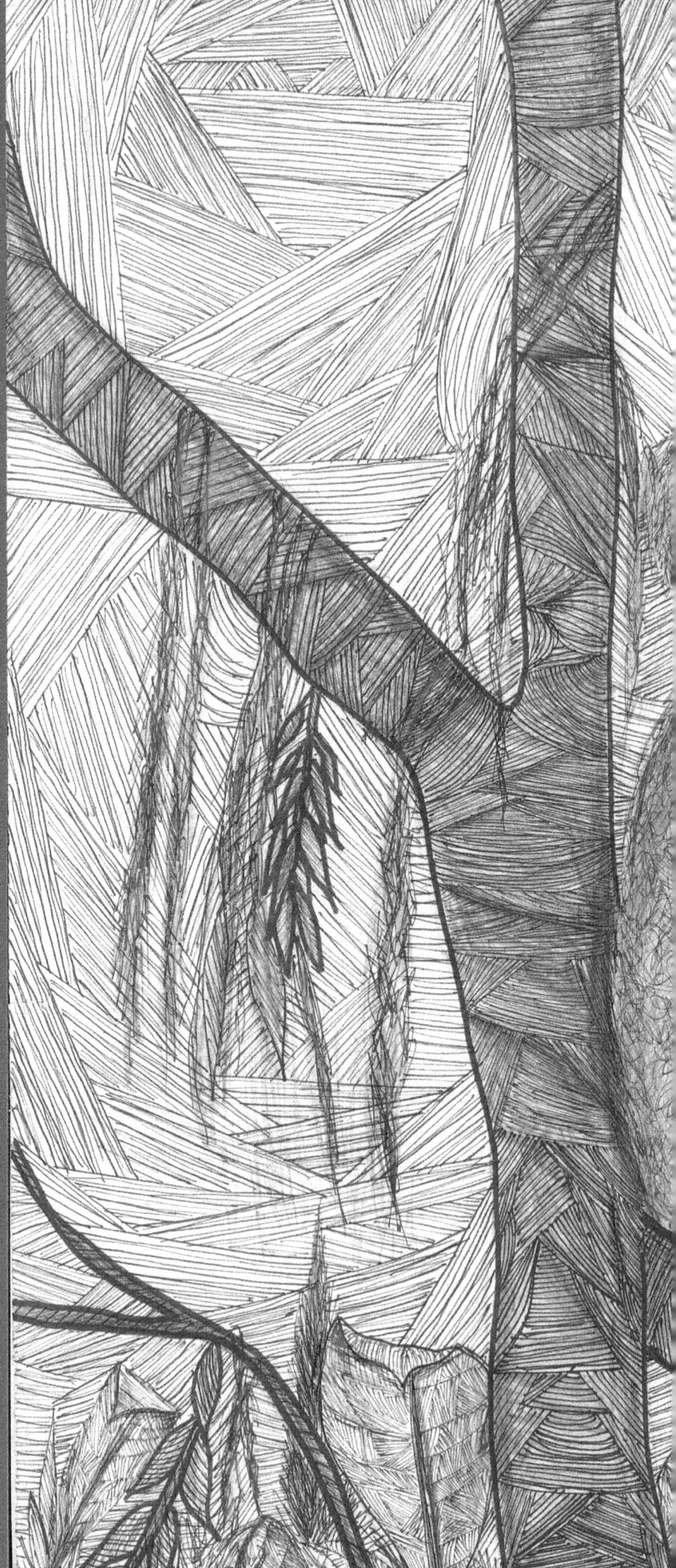

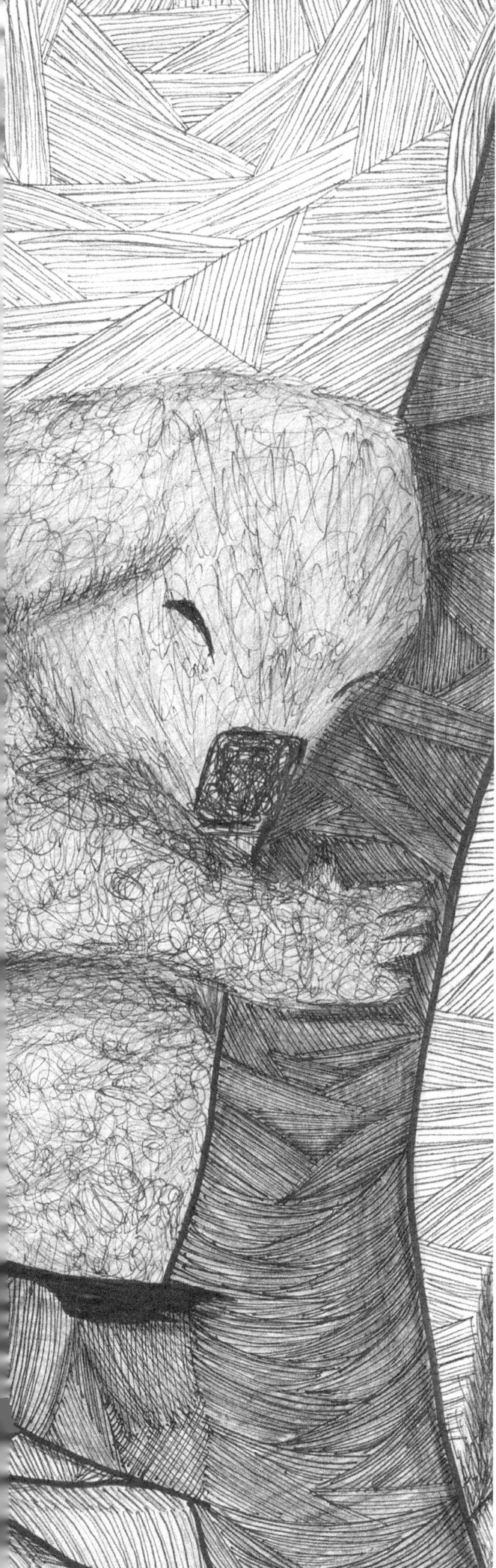

Intro

Lindsay Eland is a local author, living in Breckenridge, CO. She has published three books, favorites among middle-graders locally and around the country: *Five Times Revenge, Summer of Sundays*, and *Scones and Sensibility*, which can be found online and in bookstores everywhere.

Lindsay inspires everyone she meets with her bright eyes and positive personality. Always on the lookout for a story, and never without a pen and paper close at hand, Lindsay is an amazing role model for young authors, balancing home and creative work life, along with personal passions and pursuits such as teaching yoga and finding homes for rescue animals. She has generously gifted us with a poem to kick-off this special collection.

Yarn

By Lindsay Eland

I cannot knit.
Well, at least not any more.

I used to be able to knit a little bit, but really my husband,
even now, is much, much better than me.

But I love to watch people knit. Their fingers bobbing and
weaving, their fingers fluttering back and forth, the tapping and
clacking of the long needles together as slowly

    slowly
    slowly
    row
    after
    row
    after
    row
descends beneath the needles.

The yarn is fuzzy looking and soft, the stitches even and tight...
yet not too tight, the different colors flecked and woven into
each other forming a scarf, mittens, a hat, a blanket...helping you
keep warm against the cold.

So it's no wonder they call writing stories "spinning
a yarn." And it's really a magical phrase actually.

Creating one thing out of something else entirely.

A ball of yarn becomes a row which becomes a row which
becomes a blanket.

Chosen words become crafted sentences which become
paragraphs which become chapters which become a story.

    line
    after
    line
    after
    line

words weave in and out of each other, the different elements of
voice, character, theme, and setting flecking the story with color
and life...helping you keep warm against the cold of life.

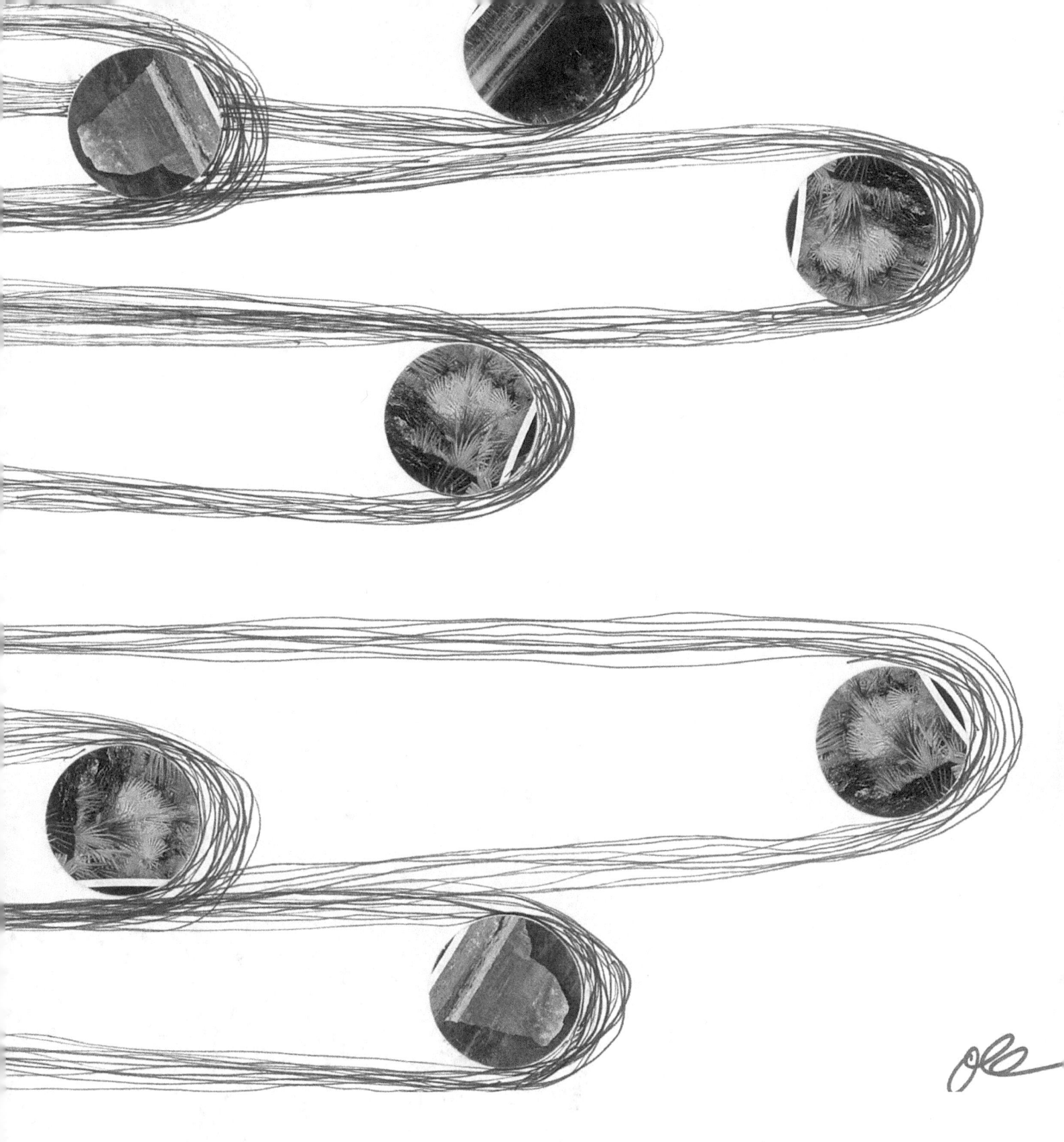

Junk Food Chimney
Mixed Media | Annika Fowles, Grade 11

The Gift of a View

**Acrylic
Matthew Shaffer,
Grade 9**

My name is Matthew Shaffer, and I'm 15 years old. I have been been painting and drawing for as long as I can remember, and it has been a big part of my life and who I have become. About 2 years ago I moved to Silverthorne, Colorado. Waking up to see these mountains every morning has been an amazing change for our family. We used to live in a small city in Virginia that lacked these amazing views. My mom's birthday was coming up, and I knew I wanted to do something special for her. I asked her what gift she would like, and her response was a painting of Red Mountain and Buffalo Mountain. This meant a lot to her because when we first moved here we were unsure that it was the right decision, but seeing these beautiful mountains every morning made her sure of our decision.

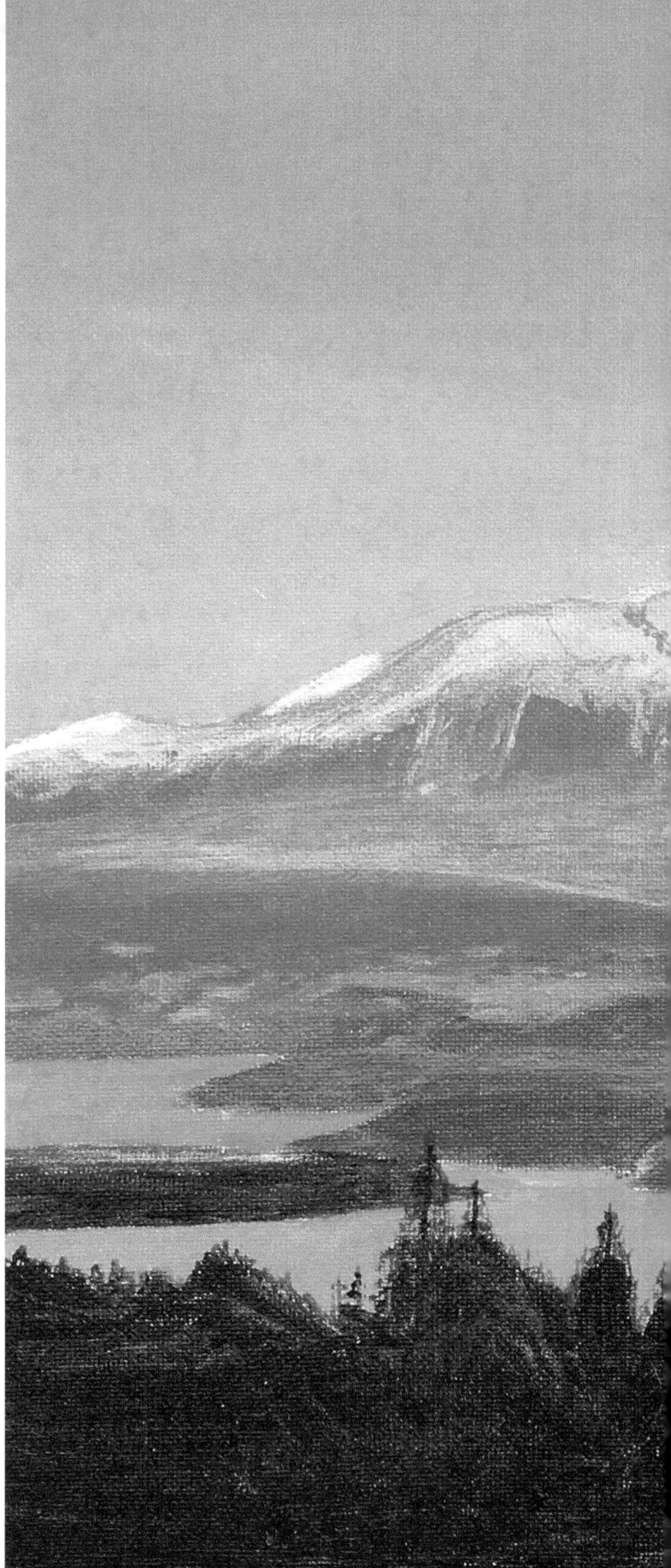

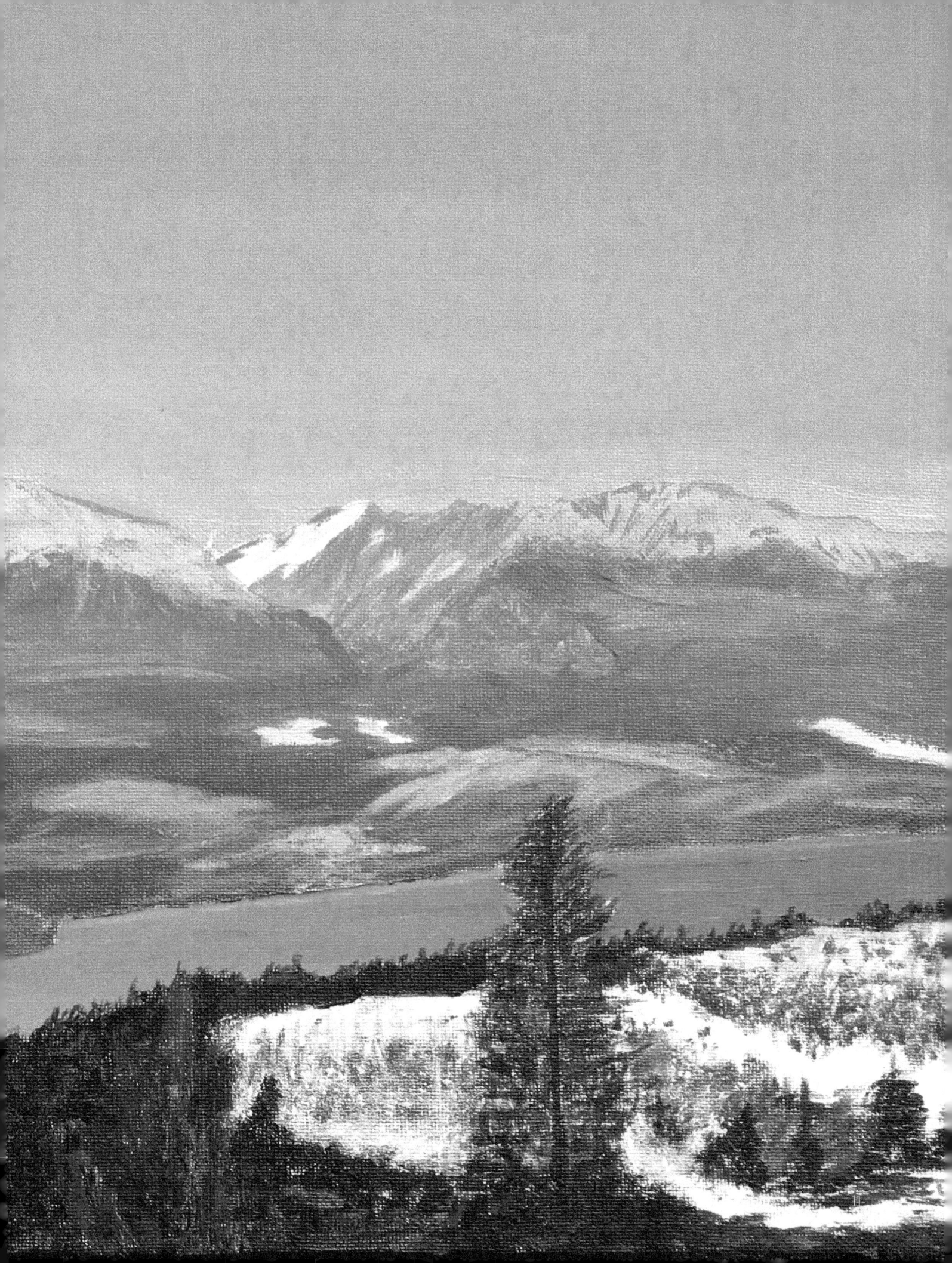

Scaredy Cat
By Hannah Silva

I've always been a scaredy cat, and I predict I always will be.

One day that thought changed, all because of my best friend in the whole wide world. Her name is Matia, or Tia for short, and she has been my blessing and curse throughout my life. She always wants to bring out the adventurous side in me whenever we are together.

It was the summer of 2016, and we were having a blast. We were spending the afternoon at Copper, just doing some fun activities, you know, like mini-golf, go-karts and bumper boats. When we were on the bumper boats, we saw someone doing zip-lining. Tia turned over to me and said,

"Hey we should go do zip-lining, it looks fun!"

"Oh, no, no, no, no, no! We ain't doing that!" I told her.

A few minutes after that conversation, we got to the docking area. Tia, the sneaky dog, went over to my mom and explained that we should do zip-lining while I was getting out of the boat. My mom was convinced, and they both persuaded me to go. So we did.

We put on armor-looking gear as if we were headed to battle. I couldn't understand how she was so happy to do something super adventurous and me, so scared.

We had to wait a few minutes to go up ourselves. A few minutes passed, and it was our turn. We walked up the stairs to at least my certain death.

Then we were on the platform. The people there hooked us onto the line. My heart was racing as the feeling of fear surrounded me. The whole place went dark for a second, then everything went back to normal.

"Good luck." Tia told me.

"Imma need that!"

3...2...1!

And we were off.

I screamed like a baby pterodactyl! Tia was screaming, too. We were screaming for different reasons.

It was only a few minutes, and we got to the other end. They unhooked us from the line. We took off our "armor" and started walking off the platform.

"That was awesome!" Tia exclaimed.

"Ya, it really was." I admitted.

I felt like I had become more courageous that day, and instead of being a scaredy cat, I was more of a slightly-adventurous person.

As we were walking off the platform, I missed a step and screamed like a little girl. Nope, still a scaredy cat.

ABOUT THE AUTHOR *My name is Hannah Silva, and I am 11 years old and in 6th Grade at Summit Middle School. I like writing, art, coding and reading. I would love to be a writer when I grow up or a coder, and try to inspire others to use their creativity to their advantage.*

Elephant
Graphite | Isaac Dalrymple, Grade 8

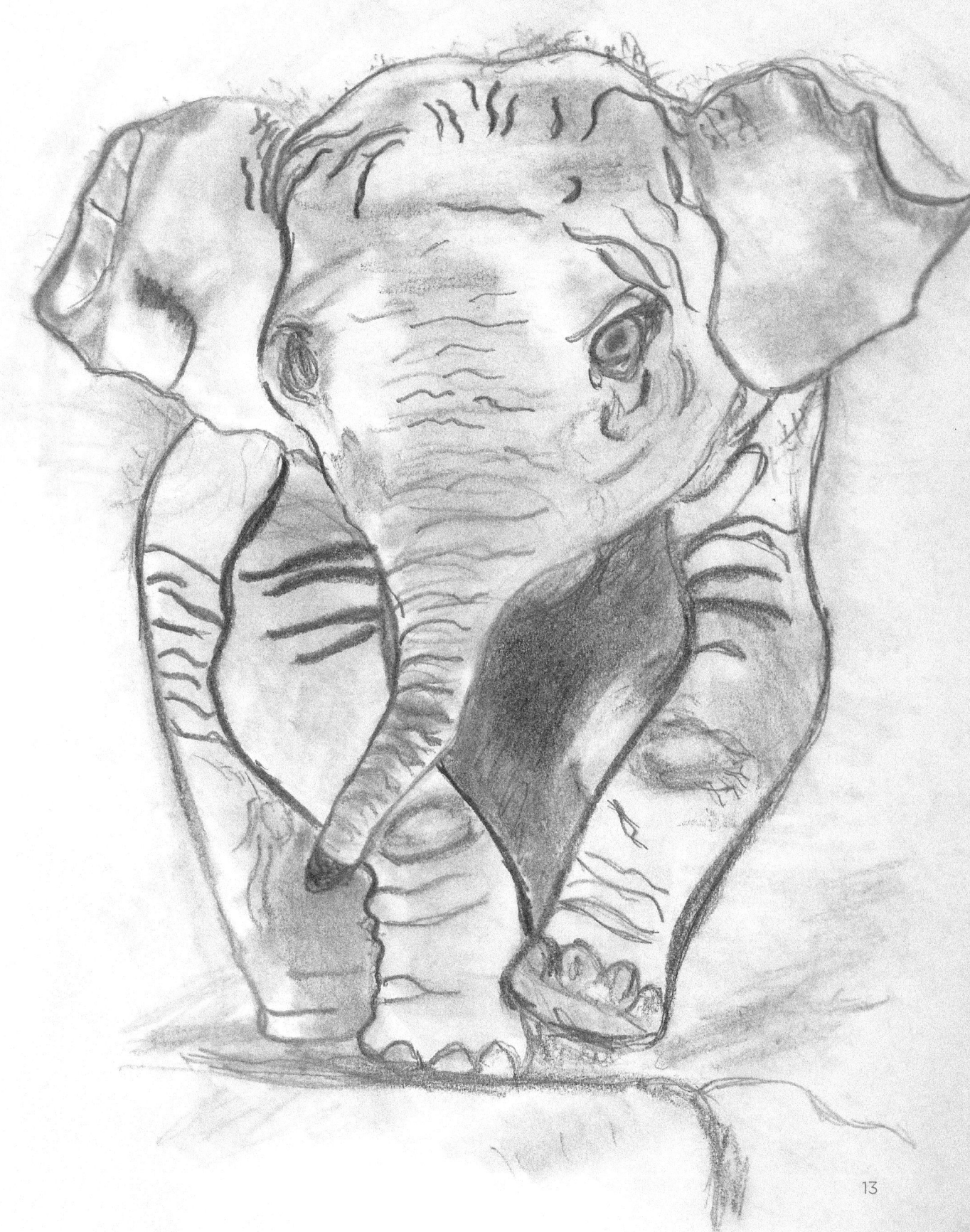

Skiing

**Photo Identity Project
Zach Nelson,
Grade 10**

I've spent my whole life in the ski town of Breckenridge, Colorado. I love skiing and being outdoors.

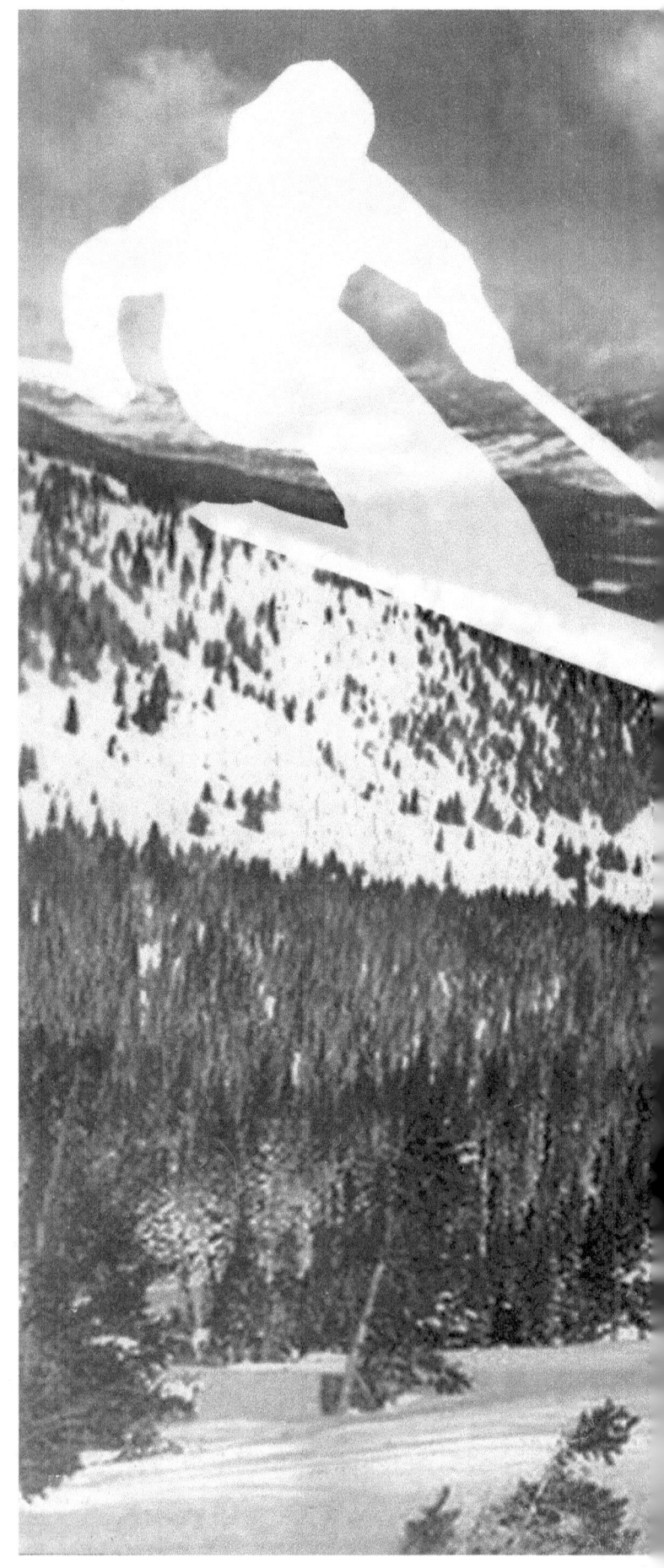

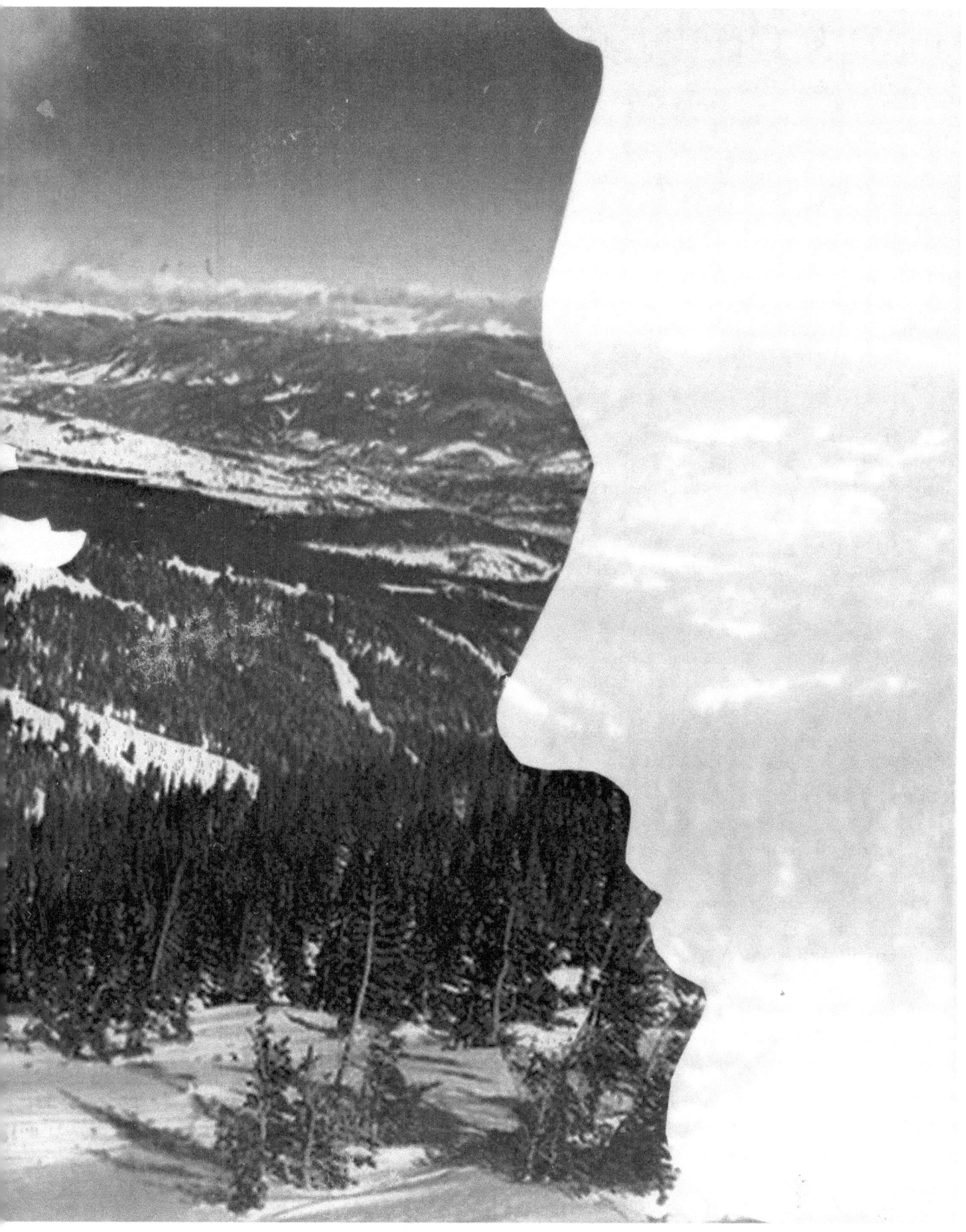

The Coming
By Juniper Lee

Chapter 1

I wander into the old house. A loose floorboard creaking, the comforting smell of old books and fresh cookies meet my nose. I look back at the yellow taxi waiting for me on the curb. Seeing the driver smile and wave reassures me. But as she pulls out and drives off, the pit of my stomach drops down to the soles of my leather boots. I watch her for as long as I can, the cab getting smaller and smaller in the distance, a plume of dust rising in its wake. I want to just run right off of that porch and yell at the taxi, telling her that I had changed my mind, that I wanted to go home. But instead I take a deep breath, paste on a timid smile, and turn around to let the wood door slam shut behind me.

As much as I want to maintain a narrow minded, "everything sucks" attitude, I have to admit, the house is amazing, vintage but somehow totally new, with little trinkets in every nook and cranny. The ceilings are adorned with massive sparkling chandeliers.

I turn a corner and come to a game area. There's a table football board and a ping pong table, board games and an empty fireplace. I stand and take it in for a second, then come to stand in front of a large mirror with lumpy bronze framing. As I look closer, I can see that the lumps are actually small animals, dragons and lions, a kitten and viper. I notice that if I let my eyes unfocus, the animals almost look to be moving.

As I move to look more closely, I catch my reflection in the mirror, I pause. Sweeping my red brown bangs away from my pale face, I practice a smile, I practice looking normal, but I've never really been able to pull off that look. I'm about to call out to see if anyone's home when I hear voices whispering in the room across from me.

"I saw the car pull up...It's a girl" whispered a boy, he sounded little, maybe 7 or 8?

"No way, there's never been a girl! Well, not since..." said someone else, he sounded about my age.

"There must be a mistake" said one, "No, Miss Krea never makes mistakes. It would be nice to have a girl anyways." said another.

I round the corner, "Who's Miss Krea?"

The boys look at me in utter shock. Even though I might sound confident, I'm actually terrified. My family is fairly rich, so I've never gone to a public school, or been around this many boys all at once. There are maybe eight to nine just standing and staring at me.

After what feels like a few minutes of total awkwardness, a nice looking boy who is about my age walks over to me and sticks out his hand. "I'm Ace, nice to meet you."

He begins introducing all the boys: Jack, who is also my age; Charlie, who is 11; Aspen, who is two years older than me and looks stern and strange-oddly uncomfortable around me; Logan, who is also my age and seems very cocky and "cool"; Tony, who is only 5; Dillon, who is a year younger than me; Noah, who is two years older than me-I can tell just by looking at him how much of a suck-up he is; and Alec, who is one year older than me.

"My name is Lenora, Nora for short, I'm 16." I smile and hold out my hand to Ace. As his hand encases mine, I feel a warm sense of belonging.

I smile and tuck my hair behind my ear, blushing only slightly. It's silent for a while until Tony, the youngest, asks me something that makes my heart skip a beat.

"So is it true? Are you one of us?" they all mumble and look away, scolding him gently, but then they pause and wait for my answer. I can tell they're all thinking it. I look up and smile.

"Maybe," I say, mysteriously. The boys just look at one another, trying to figure me out.

I'm about to ask again who Miss Krea is but I see a dark figure at the top of the stairs and assume that it's her. Once the boys notice that I'm staring behind them. They all slowly turn around. The guilty looks on their faces tell me that they probably aren't supposed to be here. Tony slowly skitters off and disappears around a corner. As she continues to make her way down the stairs, the boys part for her like a school of fish with a shark.

"Hello, Lenora. I am Miss Krea, but I'm sure the boys have told you all about me." She turns around and gives them a sinister look.

I look down and keep silent.

"Well, hello. You know, It's very nice to finally have a girl. All these boys..." she chuckles and sighs. "I'll show you to your room now."

I'm about to thank her, but a chorus of, "That's not fair! How come she gets her own room?!" And, "She can share with me!" stop me from saying anything.

Miss Krea gives them another cold look that shuts them right up, "Because she is a lady, and she needs her own personal space." I smile in my head... Miss Krea sounds like someone I might like.

"Alright, Lenora--"

I cut her off, "Oh, please call me Nora."

She nods and smiles, "Well, Nora. Here is your room, it looks a bit plain now, but every Saturday we go into town. You can buy decorations or supplies then, with a 50 dollar budget." I'm surprised. Running a place like this must pay well, not that I don't know money. "I'll leave you to get settled in then."

My room is crisp and barren. It makes me kind of sad, thinking about all the things that must fill everyone else's room. I drop my bags to the floor and look around. A wardrobe, a queen bed, faded gold curtains covering up a large window, and a navy blue desk. I'm staring out at the shimmering water, my nose almost touching the glass when I feel a tug at my shirt.

"Nora?" asks Tony.

"Yes?" I ask, still looking out the window. He doesn't say anything else, so I look back at him. I'm startled. All the other boys have assembled in my small room.

"We're gonna show you our talents now, okay?" he says. I crinkle my forehead and nod. I forgot for a moment, looking out the window, exactly who--or rather what I was. They line up, and suddenly I notice things about the boys that I hadn't before. Tony has a smudge of mud on his cheek, Jack is wearing the most ridiculous welding gloves that I have ever seen, and Alec has a small pet ferret on his shoulder.

Aspen goes first. He holds out his hand and closes his eyes. Bam. The light from the lamp on my bedside table zooms out and into the palm of his outstretched hand. He now holds a glimmering ball of dancing electricity.

"Light," he says simply. He snaps again, and light floods the room. On the outside I smile, but inside I'm going wild. I keep forgetting that I'm not the only one.

Next is Noah. He can tell when someone is lying. Apparently he's Miss Kreas right hand, good to tell when any of the boys are lying. I'll make sure to stay away from him...Then Alec goes, he can apparently communicate with animals, the reason for the ferret on his shoulder, whose name I learn is Rascal.

Then Logan goes. I try not to roll my eyes as he asks for my hand, then he tells me to look into his eyes. "Try not to faint," he says with a grin.

Suddenly I'm overcome with emotion. For

some reason, I have the urge to fall down and go to sleep. My eyelids become heavy, and I struggle to keep them open, even though I'm not tired at all. I lean backwards and then snap out of it, pulling my hand away. Apparently, he can control emotions.

Next comes Jack. He seems pretty nice, until he takes off his gloves and destroys a plant in the room. Once his hand is about an inch away, the plant frosts over. At the first touch it freezes over and crumbles to dust. Now he seems more menacing than anything.

Then comes Ace. I take a deep breath. For some reason I get all jittery around him. He holds out his hand and closes his eyes. Suddenly, I see all of my coins that I had scattered out on the table magnetize to him, one of them brushes past my auburn hair. I grin, he's like a human magnet.

Dillon can turn invisible. And Charlie and Tony haven't had their powers developed yet, but the boys say that Tony might have earth powers, and that Charlie looks like a promising shape shifter.

"Okay, your turn Nora," Jack says. They all look at me expectantly. I giggle a little. This will have been the first time I've ever shown anyone. I take a deep breath, close my eyes and snap, the room wobbles, and I suddenly disappear, reappearing again a second later in a closet. Which I appear to be stuck in. I rattle the doorknob and wait.

"Hello?" it's really dark, I can just barely make out a sliver of golden light creeping underneath the gap in the door and the wood floor. I would normally just--zap--out of here, but I haven't had much time to develop my powers, and I'm a little claustrophobic. My chest clenches up, and the room wobbles again, but I'm not teleporting anywhere, just about to faint. I have to be calm to teleport.

Suddenly, I feel the soft touch of a bony hand on my shoulder. I scream like a banshee and zap--I'm in the kitchen, I'm still freaking out, zap--in a bathroom, zap--finally I'm back in the room, my hair a mess and a look of panic on my face. There's a pause, then cheering. I look around in confusion... what?

"I was worried you weren't one of us! But I'm so glad you are!" says Tony with the most adorable little grin on his face. "Or someone who teleports!"

Alec chimes in, patting me on the back "yeah, we hardly ever have girls."

I manage a smile, then frown "Really? Why not?" I'm a little confused that there have never been girls like me, I mean, what about Miss Krea? Out of the corner of my eye I see Aspen and Noah look at each other and then back at me.

I remember, the hand, the creepy freakin' hand! I tell them all about my escapade around the house, and they all look around in confusion. I hear Tony whisper, "Is it Daria?"

"Daria? Who's--who's Daria?"

"Oh, he doesn't know what he's talking about, I think she's his imaginary friend." Noah says, smiling a plastic smile and laughing fakely.

"Uh-uh! I don't have any imaginary friends! Dari--" Aspen covers his mouth, and all the boys look at him. "Hey!" he pushes Aspen away, glaring and them storming off.

I decide not to ask now. It was obviously pretty personal, and I don't want to push my limits. But just because I don't ask Aspen... doesn't mean I can't ask Tony...

We traipse down the hallway, looking for the splintering door with fading blue paint. Finally, at the end of the hallway, I see it. A lamp mounted on the wall flickers, and I shiver. I tentatively step forward, place my hand on the polished metal knob... turn... and pull.
It's locked.

Ace steps forward, "Allow me."

He places his hand on the doorknob. I can almost hear the small clicks of the metal gears and springs inside whirring. The metal pieces slide out of the way. The door swings open suddenly, revealing--a plastic skeleton, it's arm must have fallen on me when I bumped it in the closet. I giggle.

"Guess it was just Mr. Marrow!" says Charlie. They all smile, and for the first time since I got here, I smile for real. I really think I could grow to like it here…all the boys are lovely, except maybe Logan. But even he has his charms. And I love this house, but I think there must be some sort of charm on it, because on the outside it looks simple and quaint. But I feel like on the inside, it's like a mysterious mansion.

Since I've been here, I get the feeling that something is missing, not with me, or the house, but with the boys and Miss Krea. Almost like they're grieving. The odd thing is… whenever I try to bring up why I am the only girl here, everyone either changes the subject or awkwardly shrugs their shoulders.

ABOUT THE AUTHOR *Hi! My name is Juniper M. Lee. I'm thirteen years old (going on fourteen!). I live in Breckenridge, Colorado. Some of my hobbies are skiing, mountain biking, reading, drawing, and of course, writing. When I grow up, I think that being a travel blogger or author would be a dream come true! I love writing because it is my escape, it is a place where I can get away from real life and become or create whatever I want. I've written two intros to longer books, "The Coming," a romance and fantasy story and "July 29", a mystery and suspense novel. If you like the beginnings of these, please keep an ear out for the rest of the story! However, I will warn you, neither of them are totally done, so please be patient!*

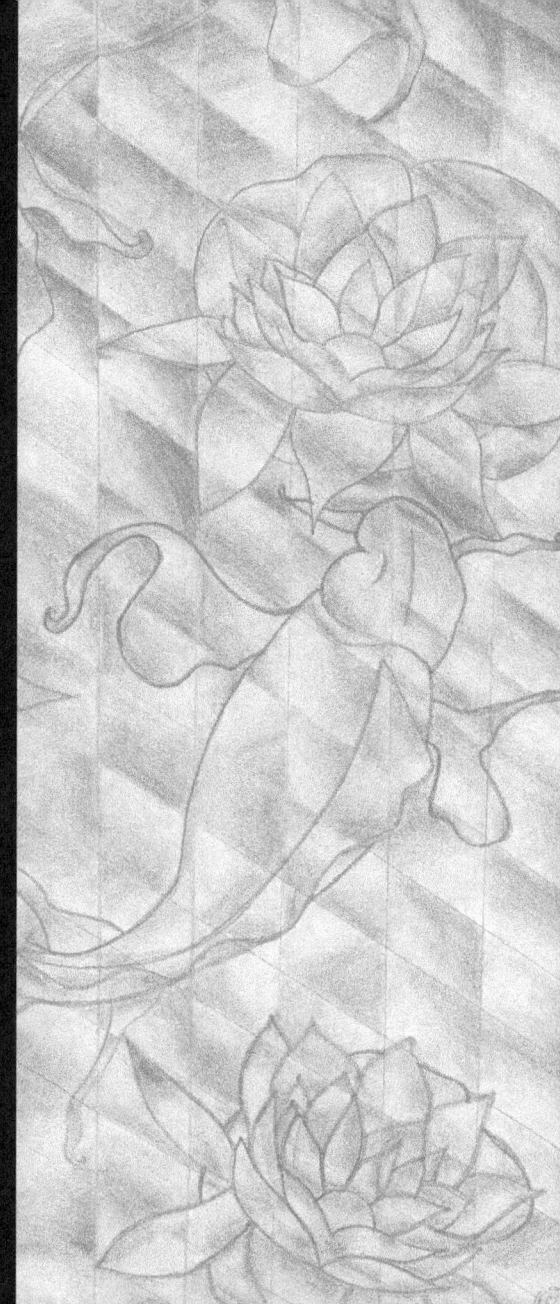

Koi Fish
Graphite | Annika Fowles, Grade 11

Hi, my name is Annika Fowles, and I was born and raised in Summit County, Colorado. I am 17 years old and began my love for art when I was 13. I enjoy all forms of art because of the meaning and creativity it can bring into someone's life. My artistic style is simplistic with pops of color, texture. Art is so important in this world these days because of issues going on and deeper meanings that need to be portrayed through art, whether it be paintings or poems or dances

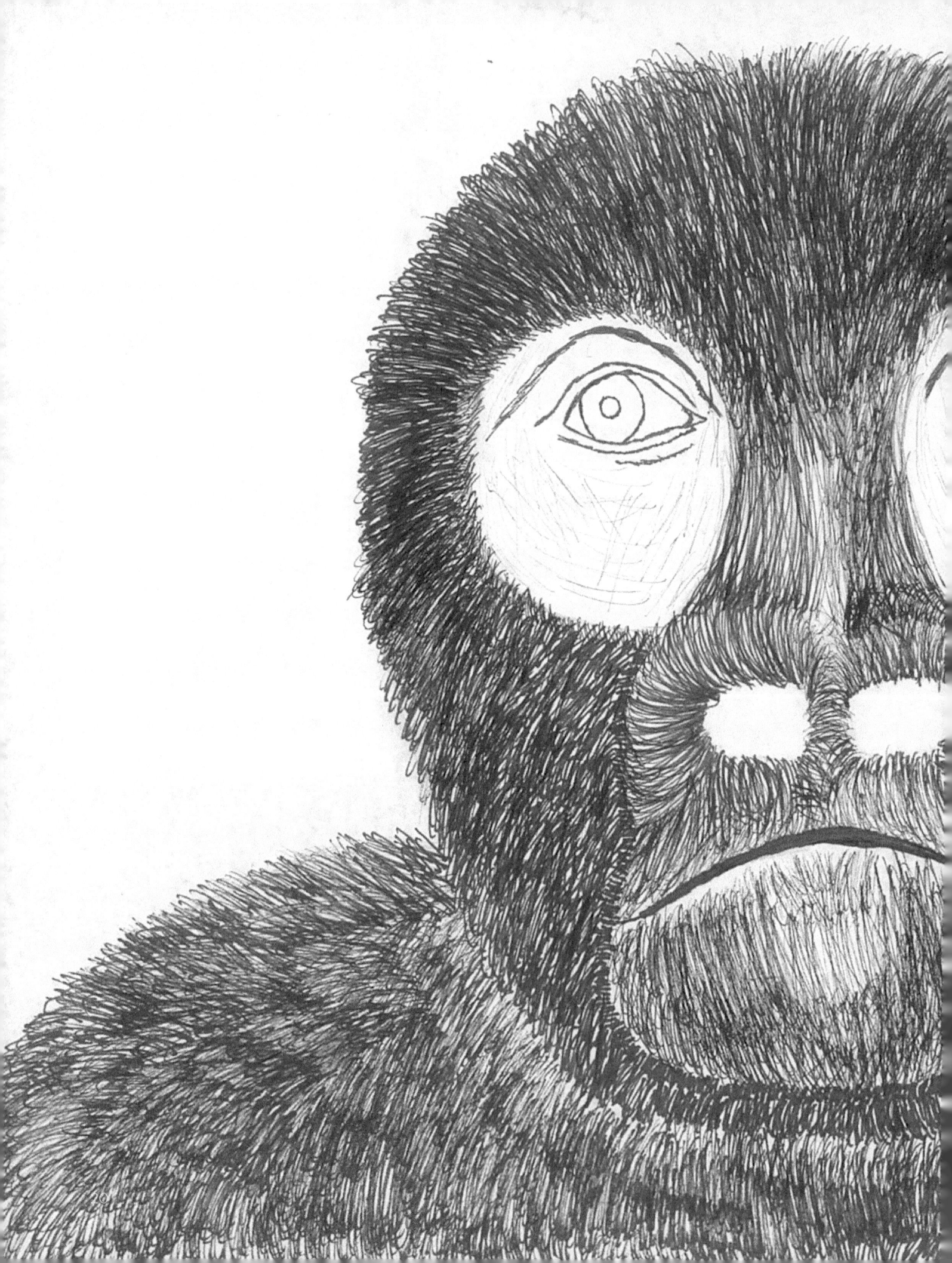

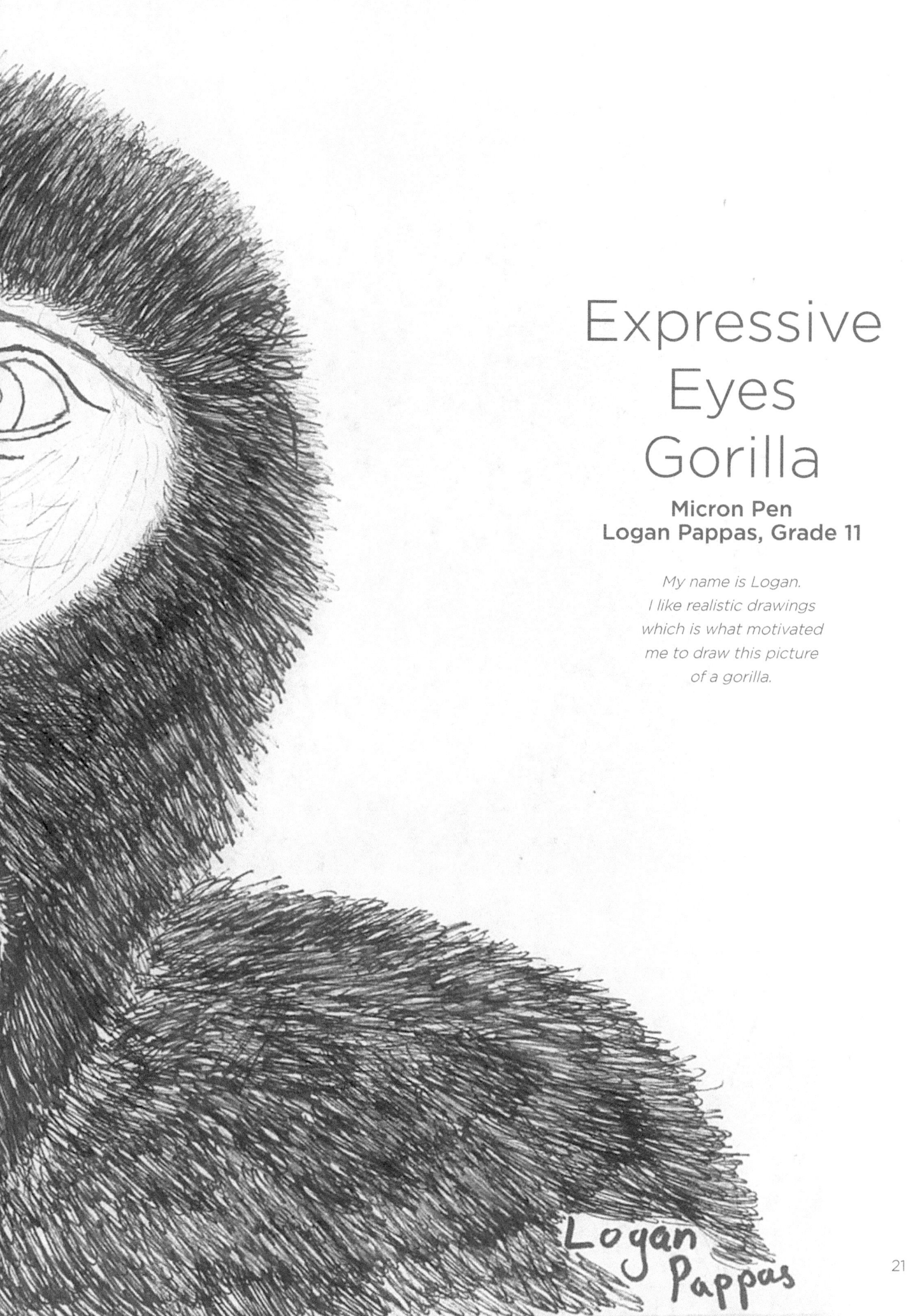

Expressive Eyes Gorilla

Micron Pen
Logan Pappas, Grade 11

My name is Logan. I like realistic drawings which is what motivated me to draw this picture of a gorilla.

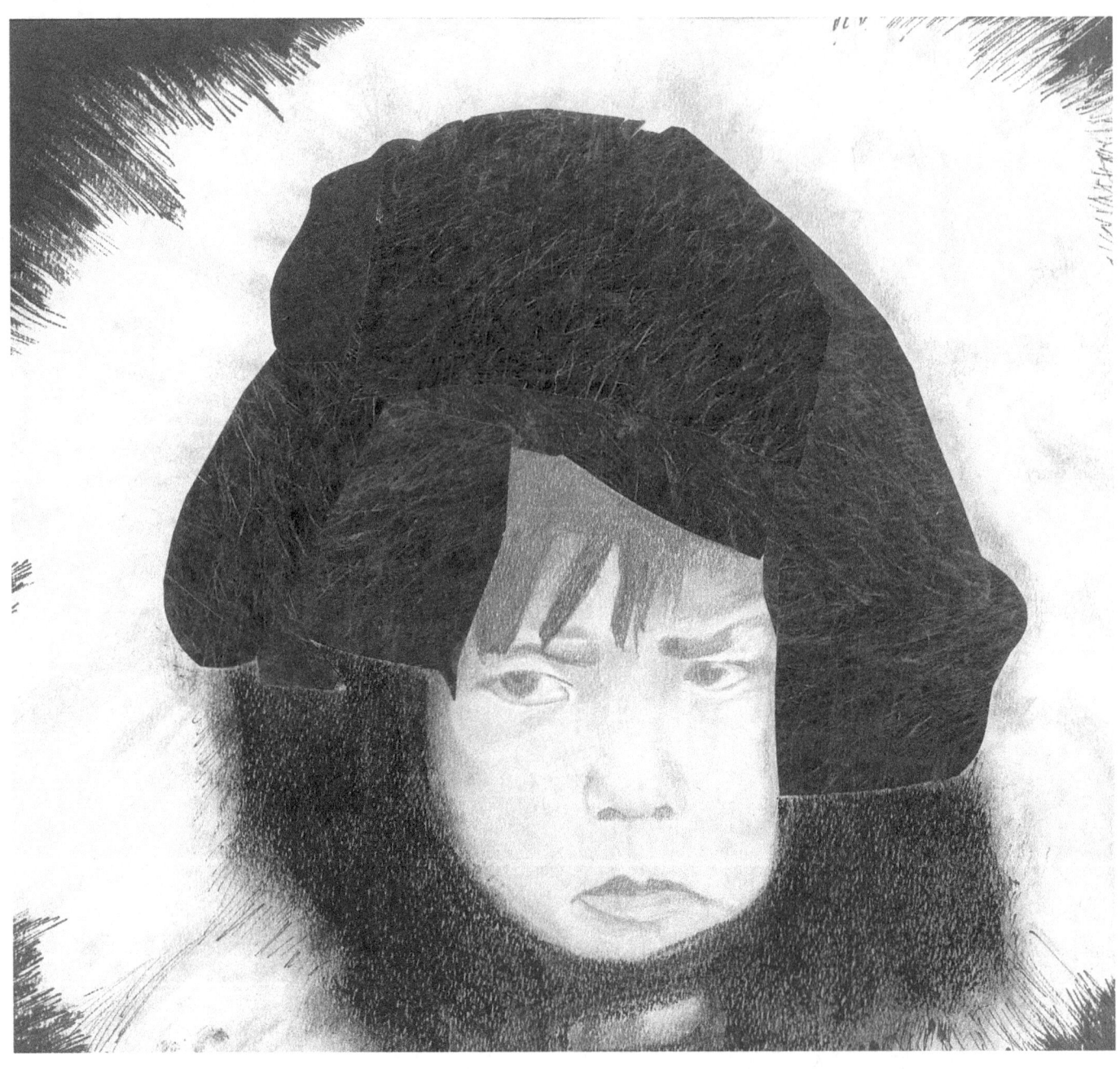

Inuit Child
Mixed Media | Littlepage Green, Grade 12

I am Littlepage Green and am a senior. I was born and raised in Breckenridge, Colorado. Throughout my school career, I have participated in art classes as well as small projects on my own since the 8th grade. My mom received a Bachelor's in art, so I have been surrounded by it my entire life. I chose drawing because it can be simplistic to make and holds beauty in that simplicity. I am influenced by a variety of different artists and their art, but not necessarily one in particular. I love the expression you can put into to your art as well as how powerful it can be without using any words. I like seeing the process through until the finished product.

If I Could Change A Day
By Jadyn Dalrymple

If I could change a day, I would change the day when my world collapsed, or so I thought it had. It was a cold, snowy day in November. Sure I had thought that my life would change a little bit that day. But I never would have thought that when I climbed in the car that morning, it would change like it did.

***

I sat in the car waiting. If my mom didn't get in the car in two minutes, I would be late to one of most exciting days of the season. The first slopestyle competition this year.

"Sorry," my mom said as she hurriedly scrambled into the car. She started the car, and we pulled out into the gloomy, snowy day. I stuck in my earbuds and looked out the window. It was about a forty minute drive, and I barely got any sleep the night before, so after a few minutes, I was fast asleep.

When we finally got there, my mom shook me awake.

Today was the day I had been training for all season. I wanted to win it all. I could feel it. I was going to do a trick that I had been practicing for months. And if I landed it, I could win the competition.

I came up to the jump. I prepared myself for the back 5, slight bend in the knees, ready to pop. Arms ready to throw the spin. And most importantly a focus to finish my trick perfectly. I went off the lip, popping as I went off. I spun, but I had thrown it so hard that I kept spinning. I over-rotated. I hit the snow.

I landed hard, hitting my shoulder and collarbone. I slid down the landing, until I came to a stop. The pain in my collarbone was increasing by the second, and I stifled a little scream. I waited for what seemed like hours, not sure if I could get up. When I tried, the pain was too great, so I just lay there. Ski patrol came skiing over to me with the sled ready. They gently took off my snowboard and laid me in the sled. They rode down, and I caught a glimpse of my mother, quickly rushing down behind me, a look of worry on her face.

They rushed me to the hospital, and the doctors checked me out. Turns out I had broken my collarbone. Badly. They told me I would be out for 8 weeks. When they told me this, I could feel the tears, pushing at my eyes, wanting to spill out like Niagara Falls. I tried to hold them back, but I couldn't. I weeped. Not because of the pain - that was manageable. No, I was weeping because of all the memories, and fun I would miss, and of course, most of all, I cried because of the practice and new tricks, that would be learned, without me.

I got into the car and looked out the window. It was still snowing. I had sat in this same seat a few hours earlier, but there was a big difference between earlier and now. Then, I had been excited and ready to put down my run. Now, I felt like my life was over.

I walked into my room and fell back onto my bed. Today had not been the day that I thought it would be. I tried to tell myself that lots of people had it a lot worse than me being out for 8 weeks from snowboarding. Most people didn't even have the opportunity to snowboard. My mom helped me get on my pajamas. I was still crying a little. Even though I didn't have it that bad, I was still very disappointed.

I woke up the next day forgetting what had happened the day before. But then I felt the pain in my collarbone, and it all came back to me. I got up and went downstairs. My mom and dad were down there, and I went and sat down with them.

"Hey," my mom said. "I met this girl a few days ago, and I thought you might like her, so I set it up so you can meet her today if you feel ok."

"I guess so," I replied.

Who knows? Maybe making a new friend who didn't snowboard would be good.

I walked into the coffee shop, and after a few minutes, I saw a girl and her mom crossing the street, and I knew that it was her. There was something about her that I just knew we'd be friends.

We stayed and talked in the coffee shop for an hour, and it turned out that we had a lot in common. I really liked her, and I was so happy to meet her. This new friend made having my broken collarbone a lot easier.

***

So yes, if I could change a day, I would change the day that I broke my collarbone. But looking back, if it didn't happen, I probably wouldn't have been able to get to know my new friend or had as much time to spend with her that winter. If I hadn't broken my collarbone, as bad as it seemed at the time, I wouldn't be where I am with snowboarding right now. When I came back from my injury, it took me a little bit of time to get over my fear of jumps and of ever doing a back 5 again, but after I got over that, I was stronger than ever and progressed like crazy.

ABOUT THE AUTHOR *My name is Jadyn Dalrymple. I'm 12 years old, and I'm in 6th grade. I love to snowboard, skateboard, rock climb, and play tennis. I have loved telling stories since I was very young. I also love to journal about my everyday life. This year, during early season of snowboarding, I broke my arm doing a front board on a rail. So this story is kind of based on that event. Breaking my arm was a little setback in my season, but it didn't mean my season was over. I managed to overcome this setback and ended getting 5th in Slopestyle at USASA Nationals.*

Tree

**Graphite
Luke Klasnick,
Homeschooled,
Age 10**

Labels
By Ella Eland

It is odd how we are labeled
Like packages
As if one word can describe
The intricate web
That lays beneath our broken surface.

So much more
By Ella Eland

I have talent,
But I have more to me, too.
I have a heart that feels,
And a mind that knows
More than just pencil on paper.
If only you could see
More than the label
Marking me as someone
Only as interesting as the design
Sketched on the paper.
I have talent,
But I am not my talent.
I am someone who cannot be
Described in one word.
Just like everyone else.

ABOUT THE AUTHOR *I love animals, art, photography, film and my friends + family. Although I am usually drawing or making DIY projects, I love to read and write as well! You can follow my artwork on Instagram @artisteland.*

Spotlight
By Anna Vos

I know that most people hate being in front of a crowd. But I have to admit, I don't hate it, I love it. I need it.

Three years ago, I started to get into acting. I had gone to an acting summer camp, and I noticed the rush of the show lit a little spark inside of me. The excitement I felt during the camp right before I got on stage was something I wanted to experience again. I was a busy 7 year old. I had something Monday through Friday every week, but I decided to join the play *A Charlie Brown Christmas*.

Now, of course, I just got the best director of all. Tim. He had a way that made everything fun. We would play games and then get to business, play games, work on the show, play games, sing. In this way, he had my 7 year old brain engaged.

I specifically remember I wanted a good role, but I didn't want the weight of the whole show to rest almost completely on me. I played the character Sally Brown, Charlie Brown's sister. Now, I realize I could have gotten a bigger role because Tim was amazing. He would have pushed me just the right way.

The play was a huge success. Kids had to sit on the floor of the stage as the theater was packed to the brim. Remember that zing I felt that summer? Well, it was right back with me during the performance. That rush of adrenaline, the heat of the bright lights being on me...I loved it.

I loved the rush I'd get while performing, and I loved having the people in the audience forget about their lives for a while and just become immersed in the life we were acting out. It's an amazing feeling, and the power of being able to bring this to people is huge.

I was so grateful to have Tim as my director, and not just because of the aspect of the games. Tim helped my love for acting root deep.

You know that feeling when you first get into something, then do it for a while and give up on it? Eventually, everything I like to do just crumples up and dies. It happened with dance, it happened with swimming, and it happened with piano.

But my love for acting is still strong. Because of Tim, it was able to really reach towards me and grab hold of my heart. I'm not saying that with time it won't fade, but it's stayed with me longer than anything else.

Someone once told me that in order to be enthusiastic about something, your teacher must be enthusiastic about it as well. Tim really fit that. It's the only thing that I still get excited about.

Maybe it's because of that zing I get when I perform, or maybe it's because of the relationship you build with your fellow actors. Maybe it's both. I don't know, but what I do know is that's all that matters for now.

Tim ended up moving away last year, but that doesn't stop me, because that love of the stage is still in me. Now, every single time I have an opportunity to get on stage, I take it.

ABOUT THE AUTHOR *I'm Anna Vos, a 6th grader at Summit Middle School. I am 11 years old. I love acting (of course), singing, reading, and hanging out with friends. I speak Czech along with English, and I own a 1 year old cat, Winnie, that can play fetch.*

Kaleidoscope Vision
Colored pencils on Artagain Paper | Ella Eland, Grade 8

I am a 14 year old 8th grader at Summit Middle School. I am a self taught artist that works mainly in colored pencil. I love drawing people, and hope to draw more pieces raising awareness on issues I am passionate about as I grow as an artist. I hope to inspire and impact people with my art. My family, specifically my mom and dad, have influenced me the most for encouraging me to keep on drawing and do what I love. You can follow my art on Instagram @artisteland

This drawing is inspired by a photo by Brighton Galvin (@brightong on Instagram)

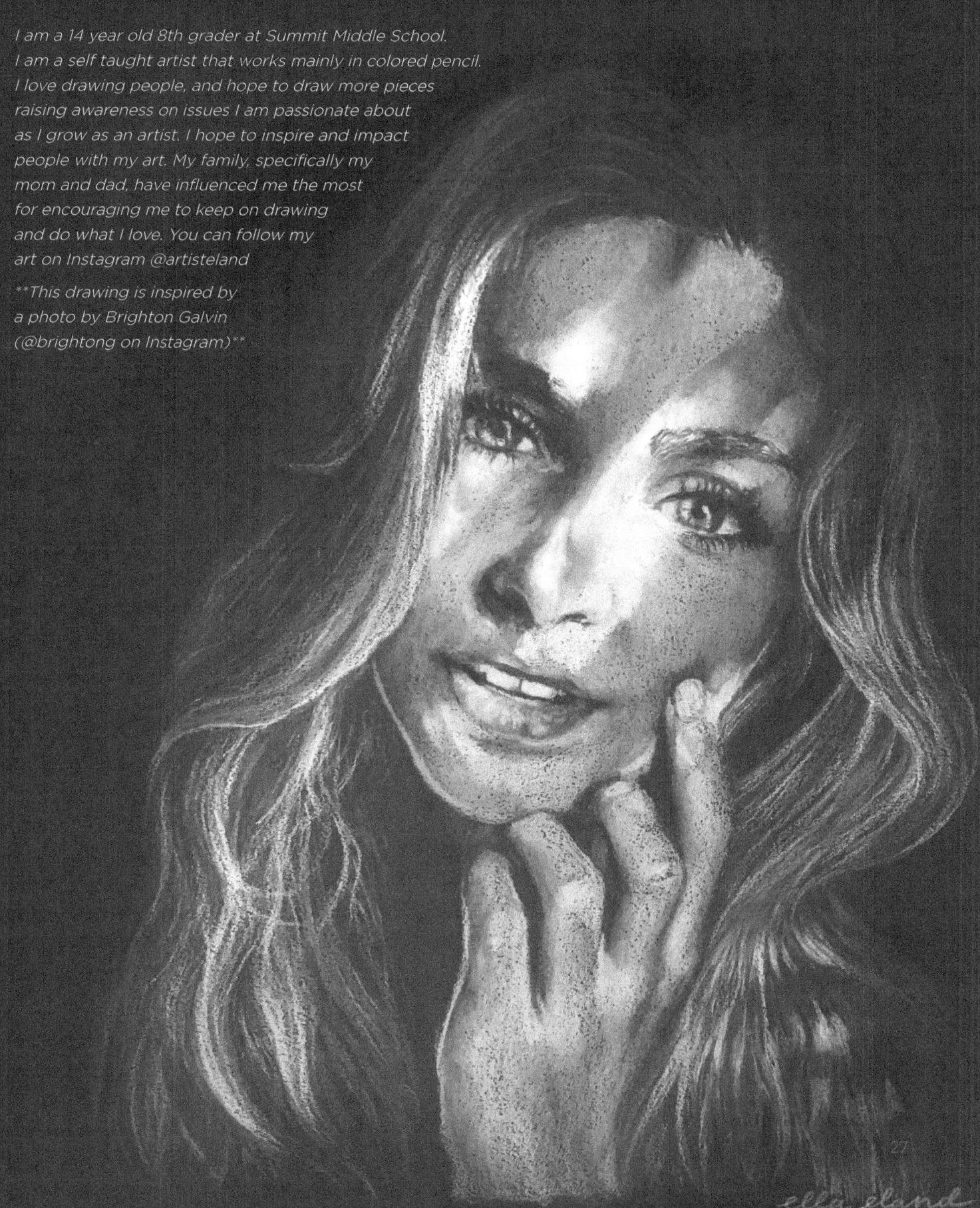

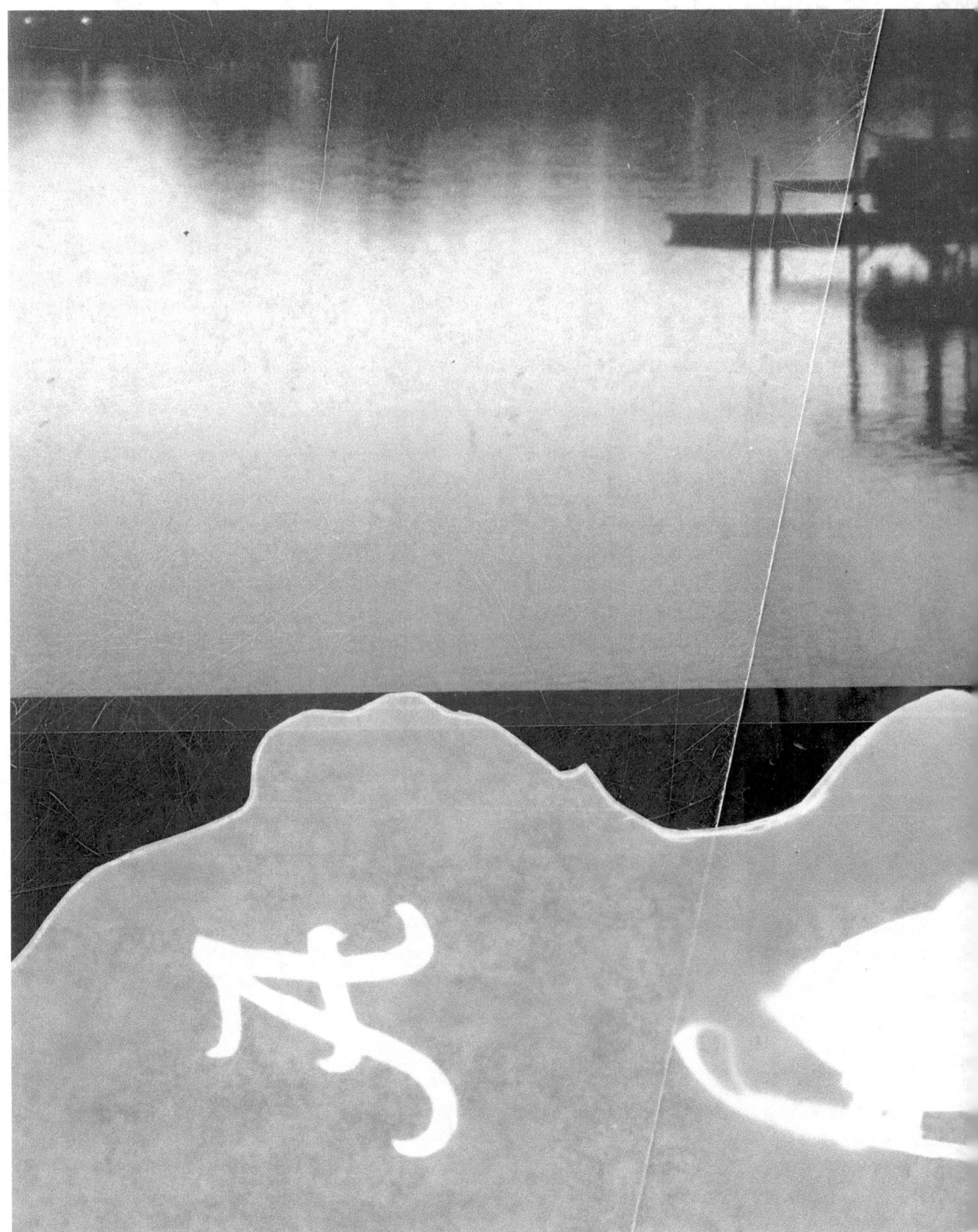

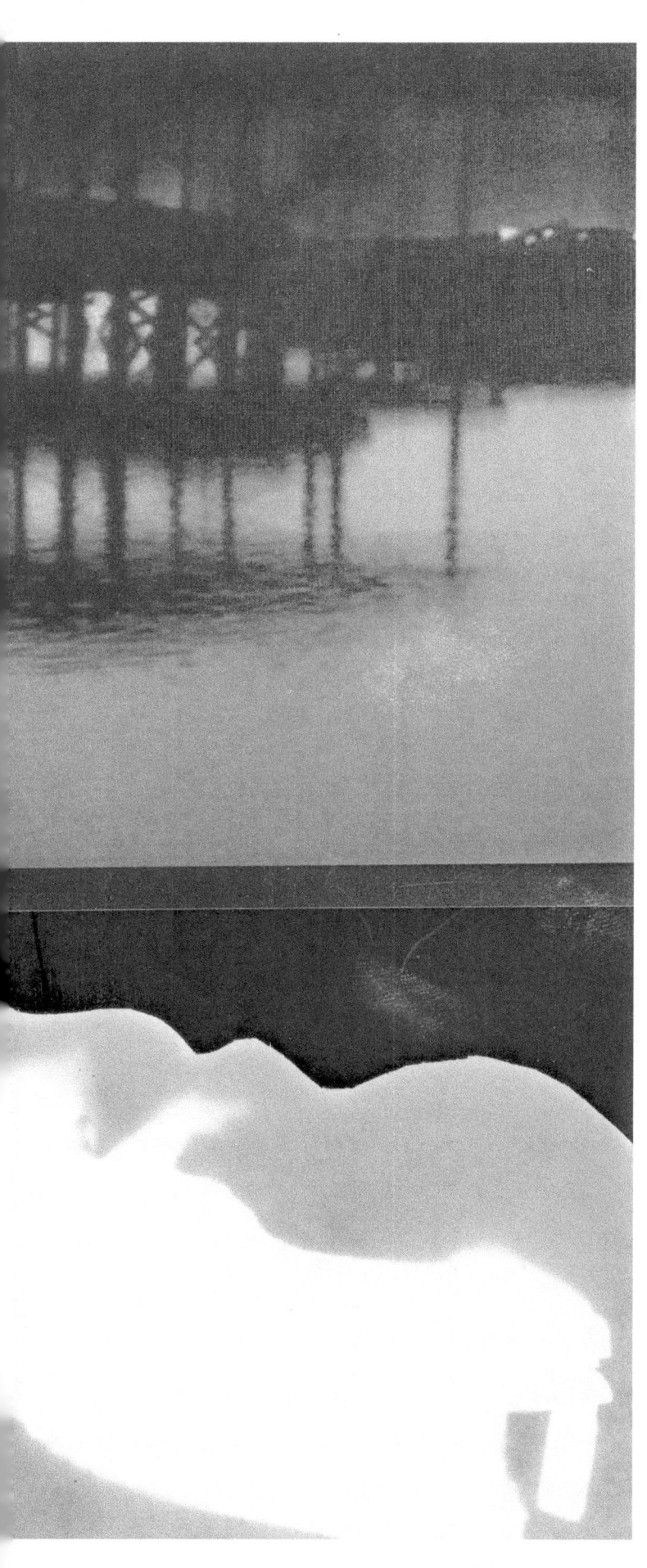

Lakes and Snowmobiles

**Silver Gelatin Print
Matthew Shuttleworth,
Grade 10**

I was born and raised in Birmingham, Alabama. I was a huge Alabama fan while growing up, and I loved going down to my family's lake house every weekend that I could. After my family moved, I became interested in snowmobiling and more outdoor things.

394 Starlet Lane
By Maggie Butler

All it was was a sprained ankle, and in the course of six hours, rumor had it that I was in the local hospital in a full body cast. How anyone thought that I could have possibly done something stupid enough to get myself plastered up from head to toe, I have no idea. Of course, in the hours that I spent curled up on our couch while icing my ankle, the teenage gossips of my small town were spreading rumors that only grew in proportion. I usually never hear ANY gossip aside from what Miss Tillie Edwards tells anyone who will listen about her niece, who apparently ran off with some artist dude and got married.

However, I do have the ability to sense when something is a little odd. And when my best friend and neighbor, Peter Shell, came knocking on my back door with a handful of dandelions, a black Star Wars t-shirt turned inside out, and a solemn expression, only to turn as pale as a sheet and faint onto the back porch when I opened the door, I knew things were certainly taking a turn for the absurd.

After drenching Peter with the hose and making sure that he had revived without injury, I tugged him into the kitchen (well, as well as I could with a wonky ankle) and demanded an explanation.

"Well, gee, Samantha, I thought you were in the hospital!" he said, anxiously grabbing a snickerdoodle from the plate Dad had set out on our kitchen table. "I never thought that you were OKAY."

"Really? Why don't you trust me? I totally would have called you if I was severely injured!" I responded, throwing my hands in the air.

"You don't have a phone," Peter said, stuffing another cookie in his mouth. "Thtibes. Ith theebs bibe thubthib oo oob oo."

"What?"

He swallowed with some difficulty. "I said, 'Besides. It seems like something you would do.' And it does. Remember that time that there was so much snow on the roof that you thought that it would be a good idea to go sledding on the roof?"

"So?" I asked defensively. "Nothing happened."

He stared at me incredulously, nicking another cookie. "Um, as I recall, you broke your arm in two places, and your parents and I were the only ones who wanted to sign your cast."

"Oh yeah," I remembered suddenly, scratching my forehead. "That was when Christie O'Donnell told everybody that I had gotten my brain transplanted with a watermelon."

Peter laughed. "No, that's when you biked into a tree in third grade."

I fixed him with my most withering gaze, which made Peter begin laughing hysterically until he nearly choked on his fifth cookie.

"Okay," I said as sternly as I could, sitting back down and moving the plate across the table, "No more cookies for you."

"Aww, man!" groaned Peter. "That's the only snack I've had since three!"

"Three was an hour ago, Peter."

"I know! That's why I'm so hungry!"

"You know, for a short skinny guy, you sure do eat a lot. Are you sure you're not a hobbit?"

Peter ignored this comment, then itched his nose and tried to grab the cookies. I pushed them away yet again. He gave an irritated huff, leaned back in his chair, and then popped back up.

"Let's go see Tess! I'm bored, and she always

lets us have cookies."

I frowned. "I'm not NOT letting you have cookies. And I have to stay here and ice my foot. According to Mom."

"Please? I'll pull you in the wagon!"

Well, it wasn't like I was going to say no.

***

"Can you get out and walk now?" whined Peter, stopping his bike for the fifth time in the past seven minutes.

"No," I said loftily, popping a red Goldfish into my mouth. "I'm rather enjoying this."

"Well, I'm not."

I rolled my eyes. "Come on! You have, like, three feet left to go and then her driveway."

"I am not pulling you up her driveway. It's too freaking steep. "

"Oh, okay," I sighed, like an old film star. "I guess I'd better just limp on the grass, then. Help me out."

Peter did as I ordered, mumbling something about friends and scruples and lack of repayment as he gave me his scrawny arm to lean on so that I could hoist myself up. I grabbed my distressed blue and brown satchel from the little red wagon, and slung it across Peter's shoulder. He looked at me, completely and totally exasperated.

"Do you have to bring the purse?"

"It's not a purse. And we've been over this. Everything I need is in there," I tossed my hair. "Unless you're too weak to carry it?"

"No!"

I smiled as he pulled the bag over his shoulder, and started off. We lurched across the lawn together, me clutching his arm dependently like a crazed ninety-year-old.

"Hurry," I said. "I wouldn't want Marie to see us and think that we're dating."

His eyes melted, and he stopped walking. "Thanks for caring."

"Well, she's your crush. And you're my best friend; why wouldn't I want your absolute happiness?"

"Now you tell me," he grumbled as a dip in the lawn sent him stumbling and me flailing.

I laughed as we gained balance again. "Just get me to the door, idiot."

He supported me until we reached our destination, a cobalt house with a sunny yellow door behind a welcome mat printed with lavender flowers. I loved this place. Here the twenty-something writer, our mentor, and friend Tessa Ainsley worked on her writing.

She was Peter's brother, Sean's, fiancée, and they had met in college a couple years ago. The first year that Sean had brought her home, Peter and I had taken an instant liking to her. She wanted to write mystery graphic novels and books for musicals and owned a typewriter, which I found insanely cool. She had bought the house on 394 Starlet Lane with her paycheck from her first book (a thrilling escapade in which a couple of actors discover the costume artist dead in a prop closet, only to discover that she wasn't really dead after all) and welcomed us in any time.

Peter reached out his free arm and pressed the shiny gold bell twice. We waited a couple seconds. I craned my head to the side and listened.

"She's here," I told Peter. "I can hear 'The Lees of Old Virginia' playing."

"Oh, good," Peter said. "I wouldn't want to have pulled you this far for nothing."

I whacked him with MY free arm. "You were doing a good deed, Petey."

"Don't call me that."

We stood in silence for a couple seconds (well, almost silence. We could still hear the soft refrains of "here a Lee, there a Lee, and everywhere a Lee, a Lee" echoing throughout the house), and then I sighed. "Let's just go in. Tess won't mind."

"I was hoping you'd say that!" Peter said, relieved. He jiggled the distressed brass knob and pushed the door open.

"Tess?" I called tentatively, taking a step inside.

"Tess, it's Sam and Peter. Can we come in?" Peter asked loudly, in my ear.

There was no reply.

"That's weird," muttered Peter.

"Do you think that something's wrong?" I questioned him, pausing in the small foyer.

"I hope not," said Peter, but he looked anxious.

"She's probably in her writing space."

"Yeah, sure."

We ventured into the depths of the house (Peter walking, me hobbling), going past the living room, past the kitchen, down a long hallway, and to the cupboard underneath the stairs, (which was Tess's working space because she said that it made her feel like Harry Potter. I had pointed out that he only lived there for the beginning of the first book, but she waved me aside and said that it made her feel magical anyway).

"Hey, Tess, it's us!" Peter said, pulling open the door. "I hope you don't mind-"

But he stopped in the middle of his sentence. Peering around the door, I could see why.

It looked like a tornado had decided to pay a visit to Starlet Lane; then had suddenly decided to spare everything on the street, excepting the cupboard under Tessa's stairs. Papers spread themselves across the floor, books were spread apart in what would have been the splits if they were human (judging upon my inability to do the splits or anything even remotely flexible, I could understand their pain), and the typewriter had dislodged some of its keys, which lay sadly on the floor like so many teeth. Peter let out a sharp cry of alarm, but I got down on my hands and knees to get a closer look.

"What happened?" Peter asked, in complete and total horror.

"I don't have a clue," I snapped, hiding my anxiety. "Who the heck do you think I am, Sherlock Holmes?"

He got down on the ground next to me and reached for Tess's copy of *Lemony Snicket: The Unauthorized Autobiography*. I slapped his hand away.

"Ow!"

"Don't touch!" I shrieked. "This is a crime scene."

His eyes, already abnormally wide, grew to the size of truck tires. "So you think that there was a crime?"

"Well, Tess is missing, and her workshop is destroyed. She left her music on, and she never leaves it on when she leaves the house. She could have been kidnapped - or worse!"

"Don't make me think about it," Peter said with a shiver. "Tess can't be dead. She's not the type to die."

"Death is inevitable," I told him flatly. "I mean, we're all going to die anyway."

He ignored me, reaching over to her typewriter. "There's a piece of paper still in here! Maybe she, you know, wrote the name of her attacker or something!"

"Good idea!" I said, letting Peter go first, as he had had the idea. He clambered over my arm, and scanned the paper. I heard him give audible gasps and one or two, "No!"s, and it went on for a couple minutes like this until I was thoroughly fed up.

"What's it say?" I asked.

"Lots!" he exclaimed. "I'm not sure if I understand it all."

"Lemme see," I told him as I crawled over.

Dear Sean, Peter, and Samantha...

I'm afraid that I cannot share the rest of the contents of that typewritten page here, mainly for confidentiality reasons, but also because Peter wrote a ten chapter book on the events of this day, that sums it up much better than I could. Suffice it to say that once we had read through it, we had a very different understanding of what our friend did for a living.

"Cool," Peter said in awe as we finished the typewritten manuscript.

"Absolutely. But do you think we should tell the police?" I asked.

"No, it seems a little messed up," Peter said seriously. "Besides, she did leave it for us."

"Right," I replied. "Well, we better take this. You pull it out, but cover your hand. I'll take some pictures."

We both achieved these tasks, then raced to the telephone to call the police.

With any luck, an investigation would soon start as to the whereabouts of Tessa Ainsley, and no one would ever know that our friend was an international spy.

ABOUT THE AUTHOR *Maggie Butler is a fourteen year-old with a penchant for writing. Penchant is a word which here means "possessing a great liking for."*

Falling

**Mixed Media
Emily Sandberg,
Grade 12**

My name is Emily Sandberg, and I am a current senior at Summit High School. I have been creating art since freshman year. My interests in art have changed over the years. I love the process and the end product of stippling. Painting with acrylic paint is also one of my favorite mediums. While working on my art, I think of the end product more than the process itself. I tend to create all of my work on a larger scale. I am an avid hockey fan, which tends to influence my art. I am also a swimmer, and like water animals, which also acts as inspiration for my work.

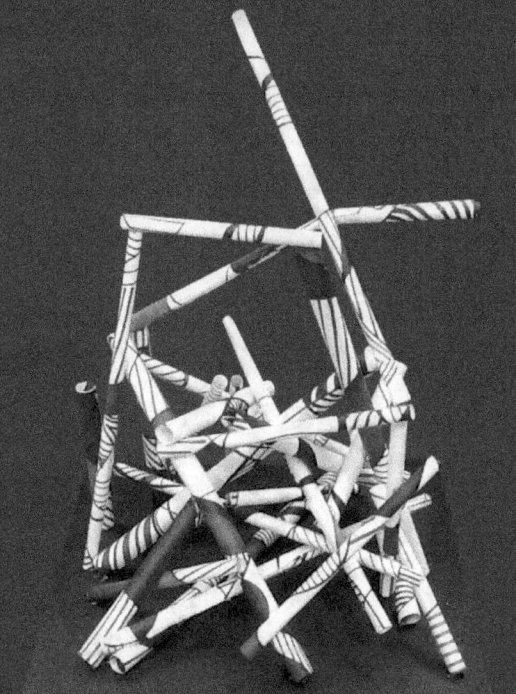

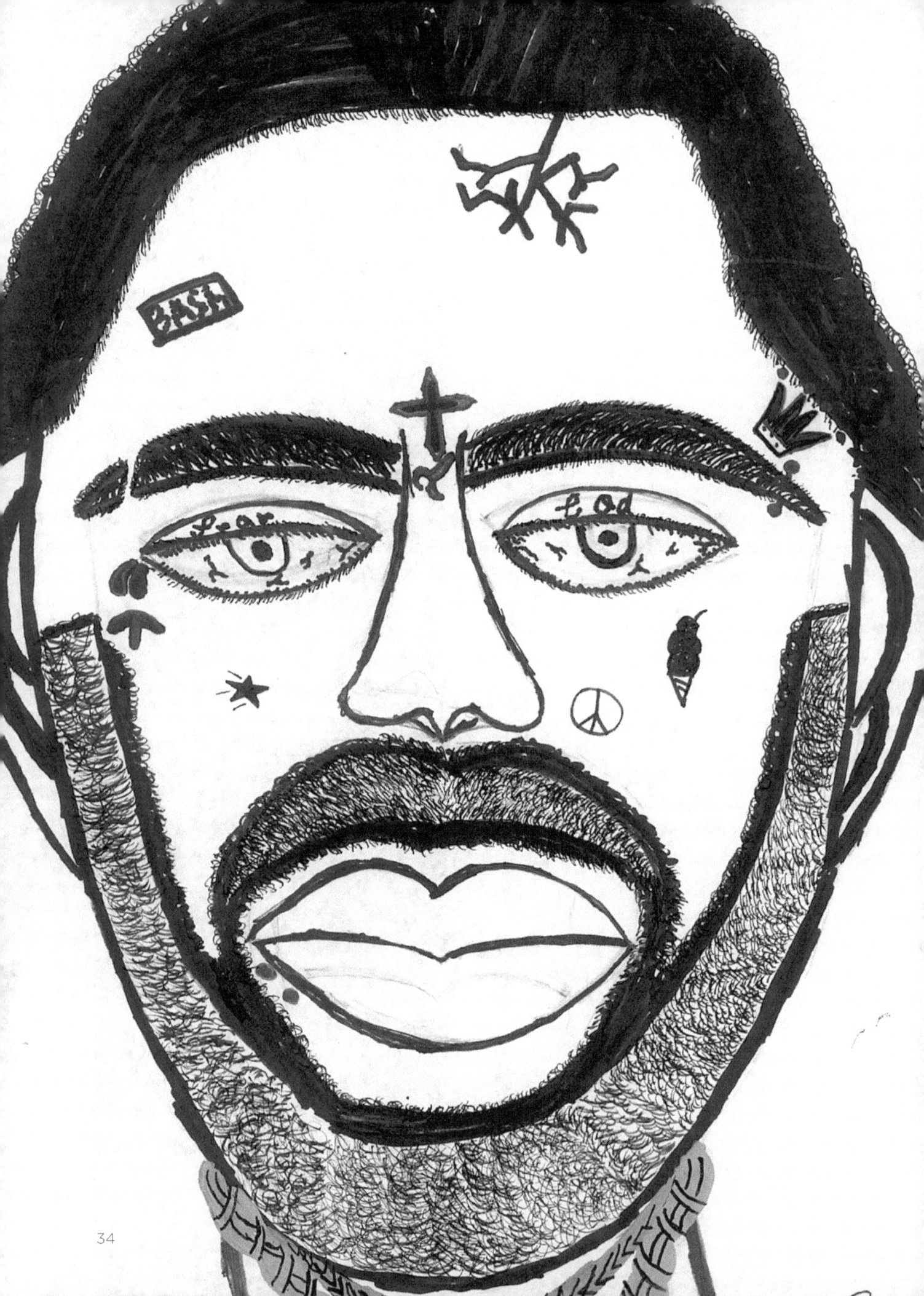

Expressive Eyes and Meaningful Tattoos
Pen and Ink | Rex Andrews, Grade 11

My Name is Rex. I currently go to Summit High School in the square state. I've lived here 17 years and have traveled to many places. I think that being to different cultures exposes you to what life really is. When I was in France, I saw many pieces of art that are priceless and noticed the different ways each piece is unique in its own way. I was inspired to try and make my own masterpieces special and unique as well.

In this drawing, I wanted to put some meaning behind something not a lot of people know about. I put in some research in tattoo meanings and why people get them. I chose these tattoos because crosses represent becoming faithful with the Lord. A peace sign because peace is something that the world has yet to receive. Tear drops for loved ones that have been killed. The Scar on the forehead because a kid that has the same scar and is getting bullied about it, and he shouldn't be the only one with one. Fear God on the eyelids because the only thing people fear in life is the unknown. The C between the eyes for his mom. The ice cream cone because there is nothing better than ice cream. I drew this to show there are meanings for everything and not all the time will you know what they are. Most people would label people with tattoos because it's something not right on their moral compass. That's why I drew this to set people on an open minded path to the world.

Life and Death of _____

By Jack Crowe

I am _____. My life began in a peaceful package, surrounded by the soft, white skin of my family.

Suddenly the package, my home, was shredded by cool, pale hands. The creepy hands stuck in and tore me away from my family. My imprisoner stabbed a cold, iron rod through my core. I was then hung by the rod above the ground where I could see the rest of my family cowering in fear of this monster.

I thought that maybe there were good things to come from being hung up, but I was wrong.

I started spinning faster and faster as my skin fell off. I was spinning so fast, I feared I would go flying off of the rod.

Suddenly, the ghostly hands tore my skin in pieces. The pain was unbearable. Then my skin was crumpled into a neat square and was crammed into a deep, dark, putrid crevice. My skin was smeared through the soil. The soil in the crevice was dark and soft. It was almost enjoyable until the revolting smell hit. When my skin was rescued from the crevice, the light must have been blinding. I did not think it could get any worse.

Then, part of me was dropped into a lake surrounded by white cliffs. With a sloshing sound, a whirlpool swallowed my skin along with the soil from the crevice.

This same thing was repeated until nothing but my brown, tubular innards were left hanging from the wretched rod. I thought that I would just be left there to rot. Compared to what would happen next, that would have been pleasant. My bare, brown innards were torn off of the rod. I thought that I was finally going to be free. Freedom and death were the most favorable options at the current moment. The pale hands threw me into a large white body bag with many other souls that were waiting to get out of this cruel punishment.

The bag was closed, and I was surrounded by the white sky. Suddenly, the sky turned black. I was surrounded by the most horrible smells known to living things. It was like all of this potential was being thrown away. I felt the world rolling away.

The light came in in a blinding fashion. Through a small hole in the sky, I saw a large green box on wheels. We went falling into the box. I passed out because of the stench in that box.

I woke up surrounded by three times the amount of lost talents. Some of them were already dead. I considered them lucky. The ground started tilting as we crashed into a chamber that radiated heat. There was a small square that we could see out of when, with a loud slam, the light went out. I heard a humming noise followed by a flickering light of all shades of red.

The light was extremely hot as it started licking my innards. I knew that I was dying. It felt like the best moment of my life, after recent events. The good parts of my life began to flash through my mind, and then I was gone.

What was I?

ABOUT THE AUTHOR *I am Jack Crowe and in the 8th grade at Summit Middle School. I'm 14 years old and have lived in Summit my whole life. I like playing sports and hanging out with friends.*

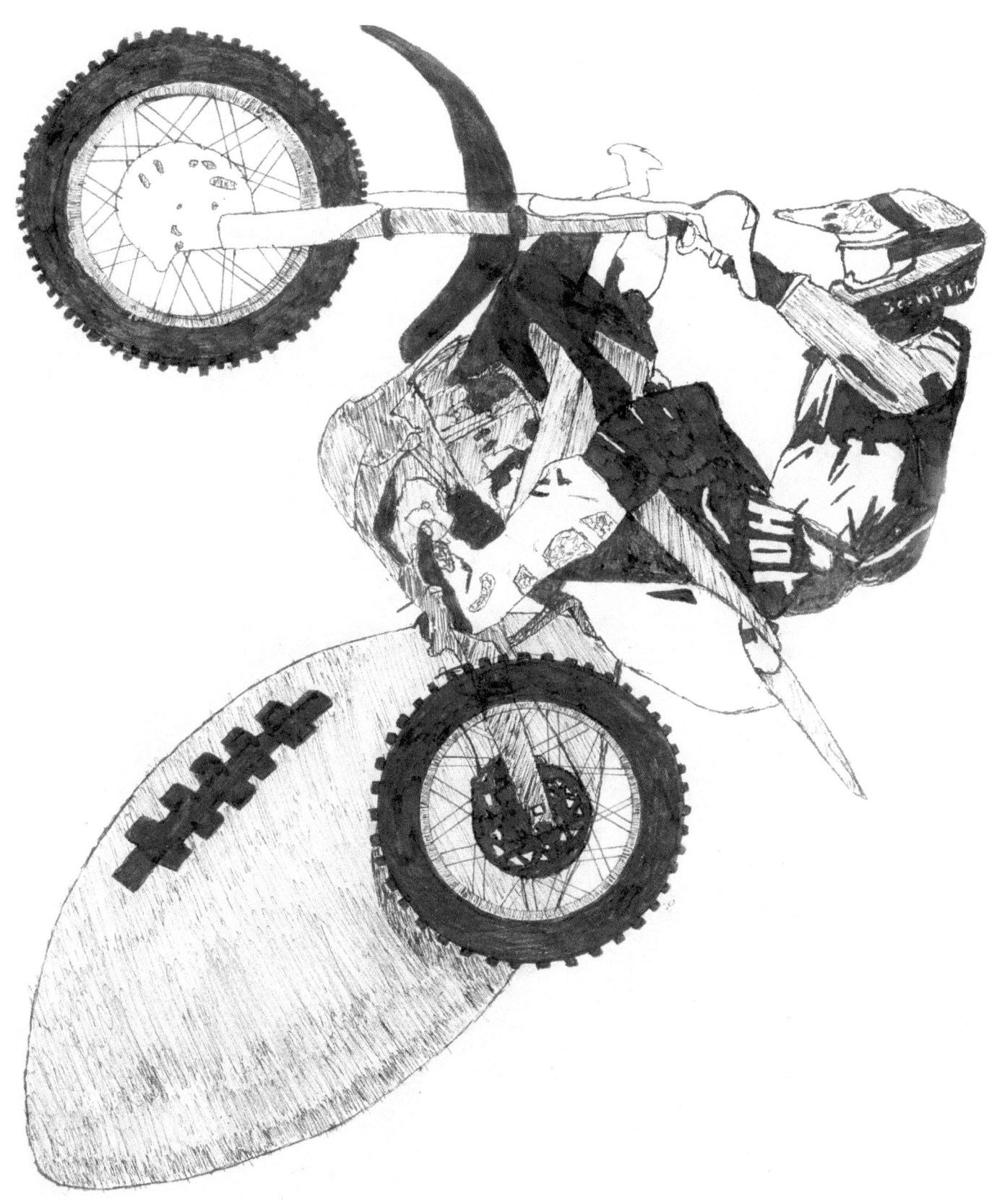

Expressive Pen Drawing
Pen | Cyle Goff, Grade 10

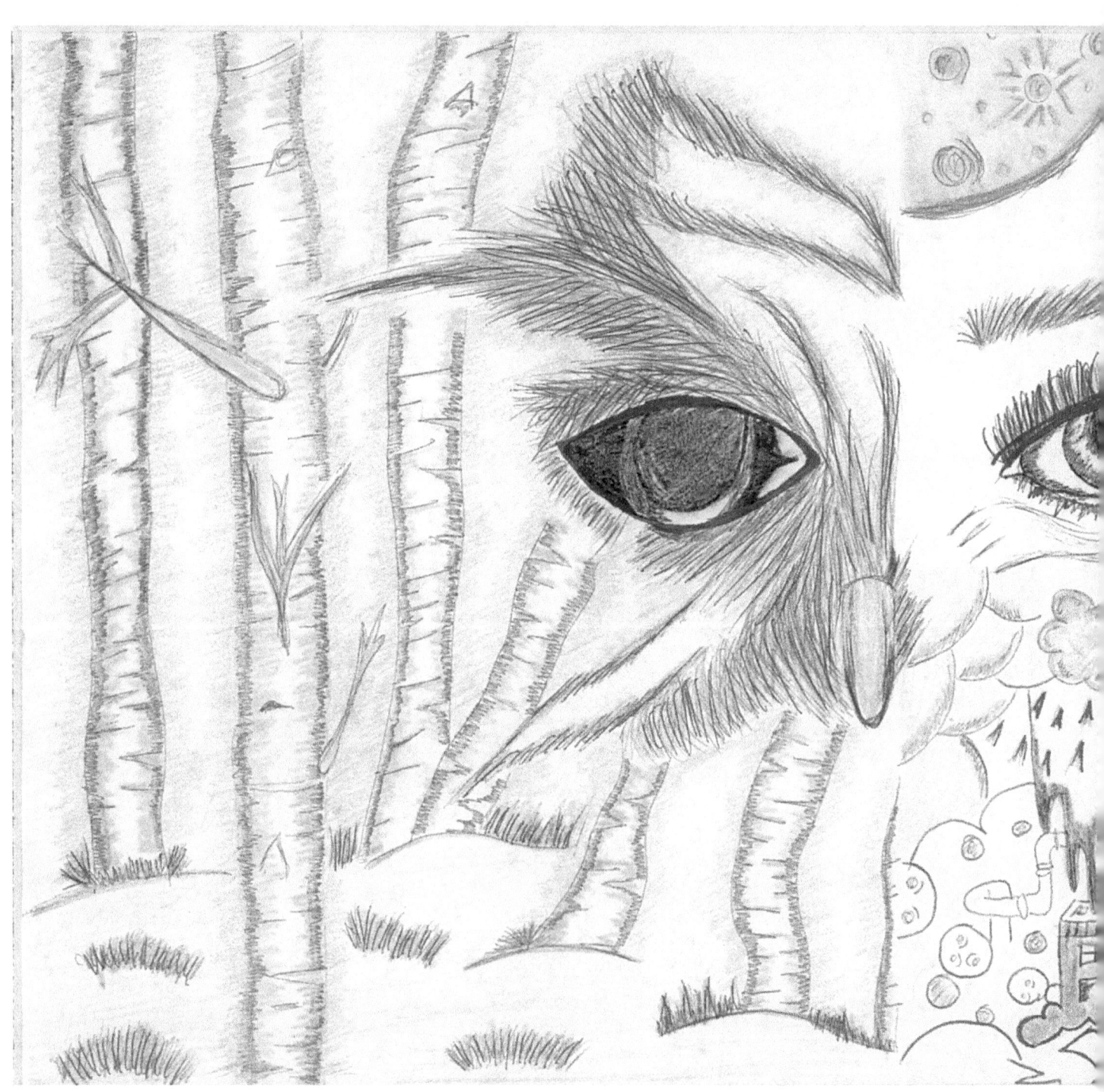

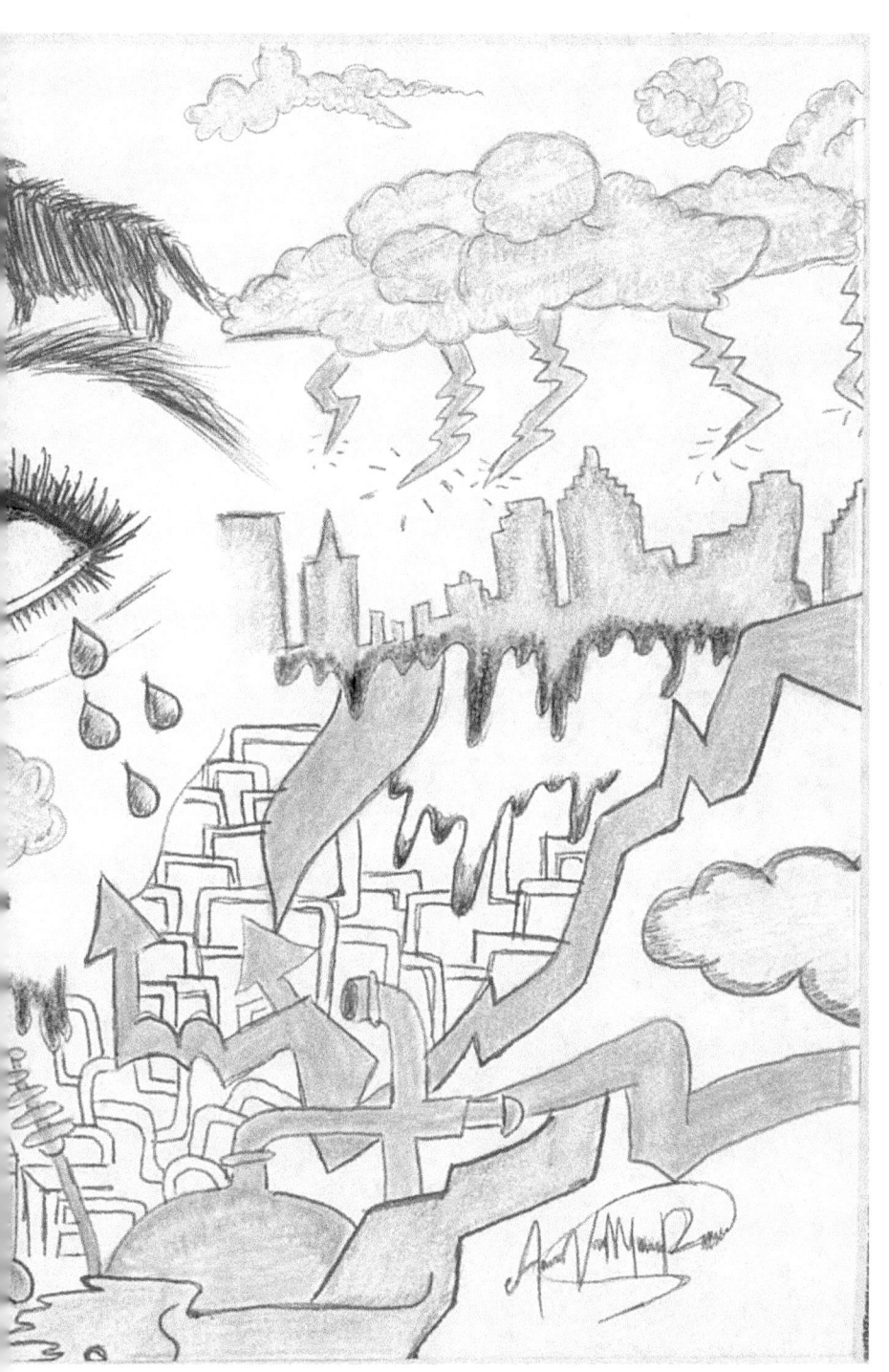

Through the Eyes

**Mixed Media
Allison Moreno Ramirez,
Grade 10**

My name is Alison Moreno. I am in the 10th grade at Summit High School, but I am originally from Omaha, Nebraska. Art is an important part of my life. Art gives me a reason to live. I love drawing because I can express myself. Art is where I belong. My art changes the way I view the world around me.

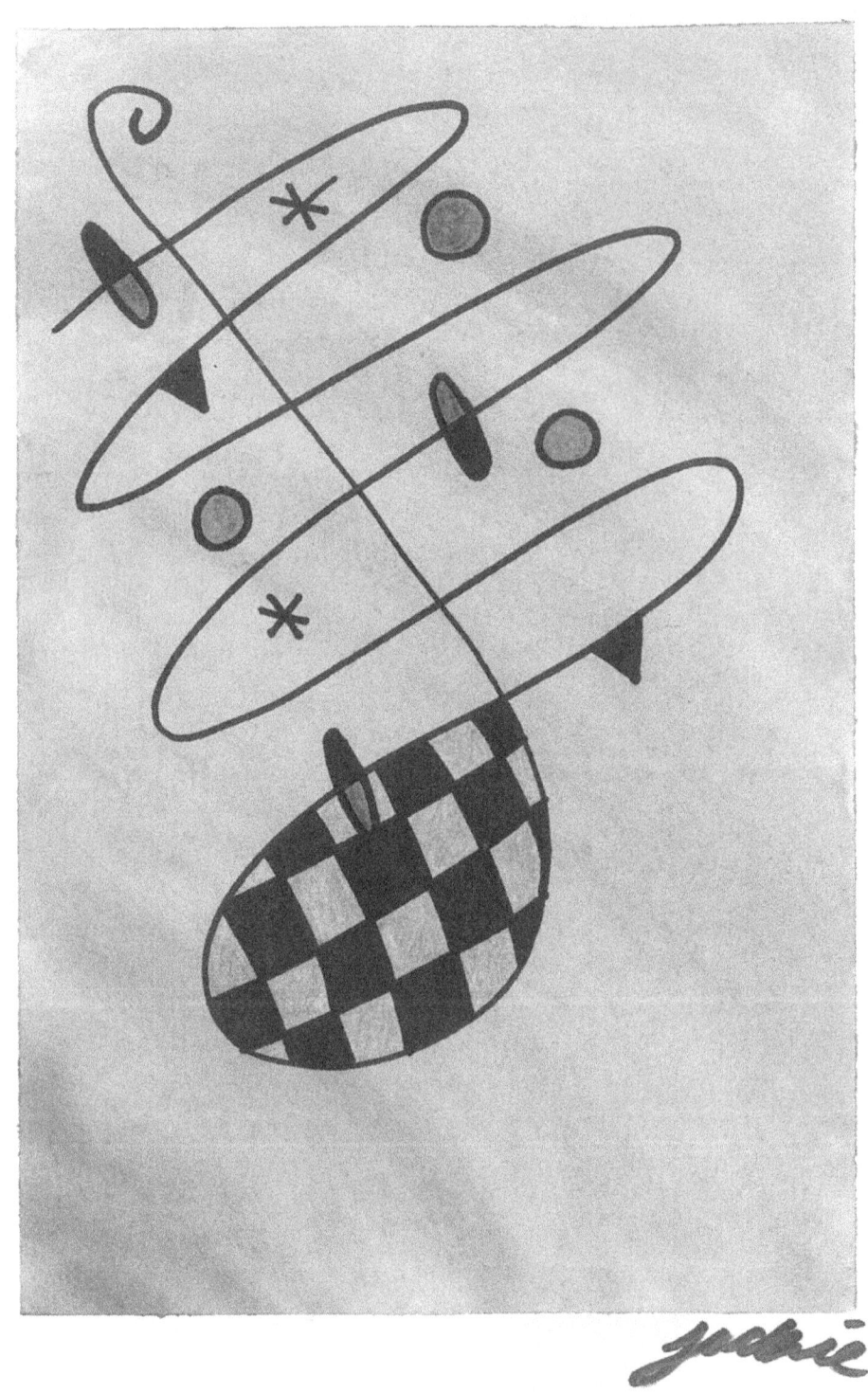

Untitled Masterpiece

Mixed Media | Jacqueline Rodriguez, Grade 11

Hi, I'm Jackie Rodriguez, and I am a Colorado native. This piece was inspired by Joan Miro. I love art because it expresses people's feelings in a non-aggressive way. When people look at my art, I want them to be inspired to do their own thing. I love to draw most of all, but I enjoy all types of art.

Ocean Vacation

By Bella Butler

"Have you ever surfed a five foot wave?" I ask. Back home, in Santa Cruz the waves can be five feet tall. I was always so envious that Brian, my older brother, was allowed to surf whatever he wanted as long as he thought it was "safe".

"Sure, I guess. Stop asking questions, Maia," Brian responds. I sigh and roll my eyes as we drive past the palm trees guiding the road. The lush green environment is so enchanting, I can't wait to be out of the car and go explore.

"How close are we?" I ask.

"I'd say maybe ten minutes away," my mom replies.

"I can't wait to be out of this car."

"You read my mind," Mom says as she looks at me in the rearview mirror.

A little while later, we pull into the hotel parking lot where my family will be staying for the rest of spring break. I jump out of the car ready to run to the nearest trail until I am reminded that my suitcase and the surfboards still have to be unloaded. I have been here many times. This trip would be my family's seventh time to Hawaii. I am so excited to go back to the private beach, challenge my brother to surfing contests, be in the water, and explore new locations with my mom. I love that feeling I get when I am there - like the water is pulling me deeper and deeper, into the horizon with the waves increasing in size and the breeze carrying the scent of saltwater through my red hair, whipping into my face. The sound of seagulls sing their song to the sky, all while the taste of seaweed lingers in my mouth.

When we get to the beach, I'm the first one out of the car. I grab my board.

"Wait up!" Mom yells.

"No need to rush, Maia." Brian is obviously taking his time.

"I'm sorry," I say. "I just want to go surfing," mostly apologizing to mom.

My eyes wander towards the ocean, and I remember my mom's comparison of the ocean to a jar of blue glitter. It especially looks like that today.

"Mom, can we please go further out this time?" I plead.

"Only if you think you can handle bigger waves."

"I think I am ready."

We walk towards the water, and I start to sink into the sloppy wet sand. As the water reaches up to my knees, I lay my board down and connect the strap to my ankle so it won't float away if I fall off my board. I get into the paddling position so we can swim over to the first waves. Mom and Brian do the same.

"Let's go over to that one," mom says, pointing to a wave starting to form about thirty feet ahead of us. As I start to go up the wave, it turns out my board isn't steadied yet, and I fall off backwards making a huge splash. I swim up out of the water and regain control of my board.

"Here comes a bigger one guys, brace yourselves. I don't want anyone getting hurt." Mom says, sounding worried.

"Don't worry, mom." I reply, "I just need to focus, and I will be fine."

"We've got this," Brian adds.

The wave is rapidly approaching. I see my family paddle towards it, and I follow. The closer I get, the more I realize that this wave is a lot bigger than I expected. My eyes start searching for my mom, but she is already transitioning to standing.

I never thought that things actually slow down in situations like this, but that is how I feel. I am in the middle of the wave, not using proper form, and the crest of the wave crashes down on me in one, horrifying, rush of water.

"Mom!" I scream. The water is pushing me down farther and farther with every second. I'm spinning and spinning with the current. I try to open my eyes for a split second, but the water snaps my eyelids back down again, and the salt water stings my already bloodshot eyes.

As the water calms down, I feel an opening to swim to the surface. I start to reach for my foot to find my board, but it is nowhere to be seen. My board is gone! I start to mourn the board, but I'm sinking fast and need to get to the surface. Once I feel my face escape the water, I gasp, taking in as much air as possible. I look around for mom or Brian, but they are nowhere to be seen.

I start to cry, the tears slowly dripping down my face. Another wave is forming in front of me, but I'm more concerned about my mom. I wipe my tears as the wave slams into me. I try to dive under this sudden wave, but my breath is limited, and I get stuck rolling around again under the force of the water. Testing my strength, I try to swim up to surface without using all the rest of my energy. Just then, I feel a forceful tug on my foot and I find myself getting swept back into the water instantly. I have no oxygen, and my heart skipped a beat. Whatever is on my foot is so strong and powerful I cannot get away. It pulls me faster and farther away into the sea. The shock makes me gasp, and more air escapes my lungs. I want to scream.

My foot has gone numb, and I notice a large, dark figure in the distance. Anything and everything I see is a rushed blur as I am swept past it. I feel like the water is closing in on my lungs and the pressure of the ocean is pressing in on my rib cage. I am imagining myself going pale, my life starting to pass before my eyes. Sudden memories float into my head. Memories from when I was very small to the past thirty seconds underwater. Meanwhile, the large object is a few feet ahead and I know it isn't a sea creature. It is stationary, a cliff. This might be the worst idea I've ever had, but it is the only one I have.

So, in that split second of opportunity, I grab onto it. I jerk my arms toward the rough edge and lock my fingers onto the cliff's side. It feels as though I am being ripped in half. I am ripped violently out of the riptide. I hear a loud crack and a splitting pain in my forehead just before my eyelids close and I am knocked unconscious.

***

My eyelids start to rise wearily, waking me up from the darkness. The pain in my fingers is terrible. All I can feel is my heartbeat dancing through my veins. The sun, blinds me, and I try to lift my arm to block the rays. When I attempt this, it feels like every muscle in my body is screaming in agony.

"I think she is awake!" someone shouts. Their voice rings loudly in my head.

"Let me see her!" A familiar voice answers back in tears, "Maia, are you okay?"

"Mmmmm," I manage to mumble.

"Well, she is conscious," replies a woman's voice. A cold hand is placed on my forehead. My brain feels as though it has been shattered into a thousand pieces.

"It's okay, Maia," I hear Brian say, "I'm here, and you're on a lifeboat headed back to shore, okay."

"Sweetie, you hit yourself pretty badly. From the looks of it, I'd say most of your fingers are broken, and your forehead is completely bruised," says the woman, sounding concerned.

After that, I find myself going in and out of consciousness over and over again. I am woken up again by the strange woman and Brian, who are trying to lift me onto what looks like Brian's surfboard. They use it as a stretcher to get me out of the lifeboat.

Eventually, they set me down by what looks like a telephone booth and frantically call an ambulance. Brian hangs up the phone and thanks the woman who helped us. When the ambulance arrives, they take me off the board and load me into the back of the vehicle. My muscles ache at every contact. The paramedics close the door. Brian and my mom sit beside me.

"Is my daughter okay?" Mom asks, panicked looking at the paramedic driving the ambulance.

"It is a good sign she is conscious. The hospital is ready for her."

"Thank you." Then she whispers in my ear, "I love you."

One of the only things I remember from this ambulance ride is waking up to the sounds of my Mom and Brian.

"We are never going that far out again," Mom whispers with a shaky voice, pretending to be calm.

"Agreed," responds Brian.

"That wave split us up so much I couldn't find either of you," Mom sounding like she is choking back tears.

"Thank goodness for those girls going fishing who were willing to help us," sighs Brian.

"I'm just glad you found her." Mom replies as she smiles down at me, blinking away her tears.

I couldn't believe this day, how lucky I am that Brian found me. I might annoy him sometimes, but now I know he is looking out for me, too. Even if he doesn't show it like mom does. I can see the red and blue lights flash outside of the windows as we rush back down the road lined by palm trees.

ABOUT THE AUTHOR *My name is Isabel Butler. I am a Summit County, Colorado Native. I have lived in Silverthorne my whole 14 years. Writing stories has been my favorite hobby ever since I was seven years old, and I hope my future career involves writing. I believe here in Middle School, my writing skills have grown especially from the help of my teachers Ms. Monore and Ms. Stark. My favorite class in school is Language Arts, and my favorite unit has always been the poetry or narrative units. Some of my other hobbies and favorite things to do are skiing, reading, biking, and drawing. All of these activities allow me to express myself and any creative ideas and come up with new ones.*

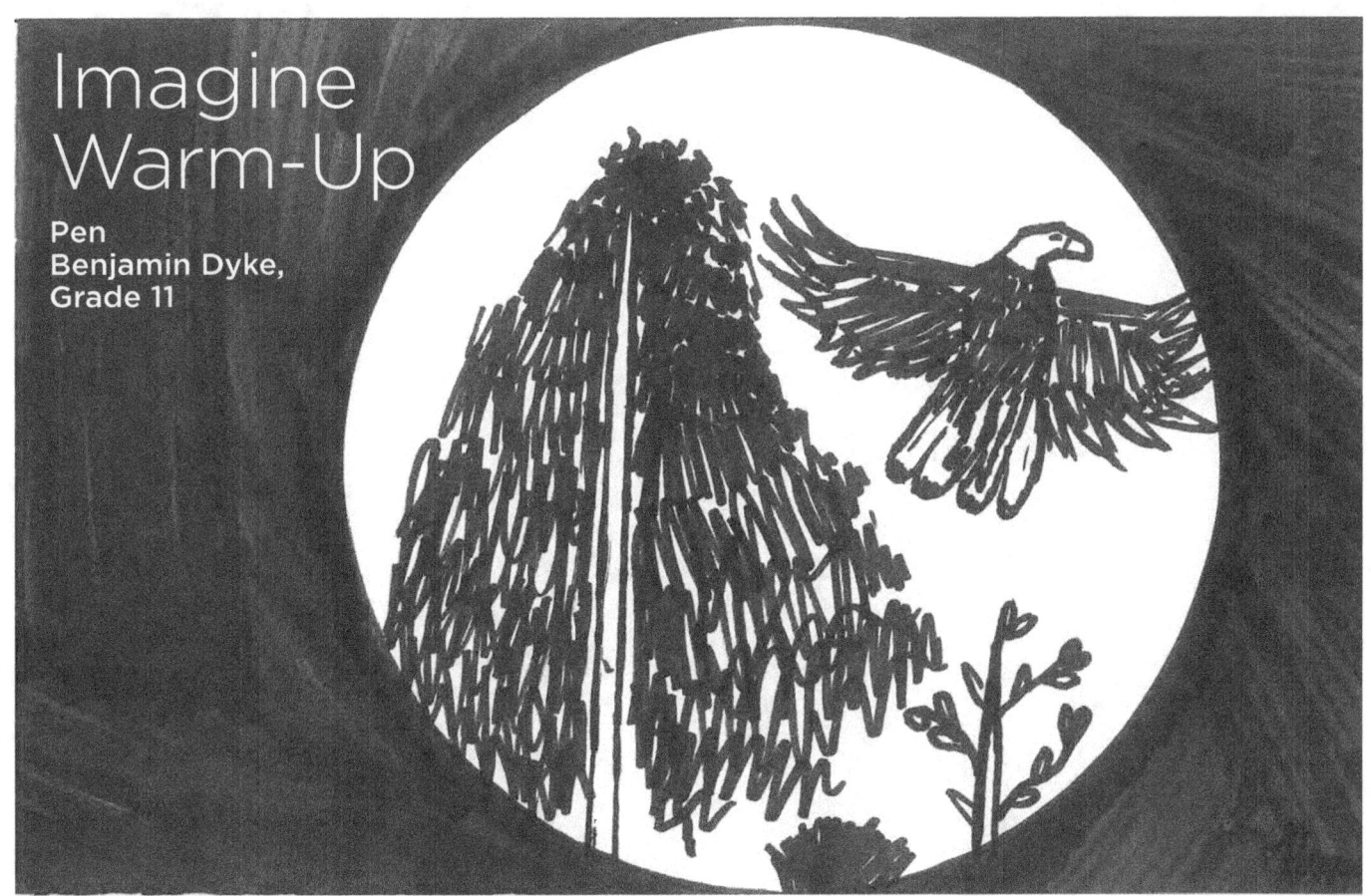

Imagine Warm-Up

Pen
Benjamin Dyke, Grade 11

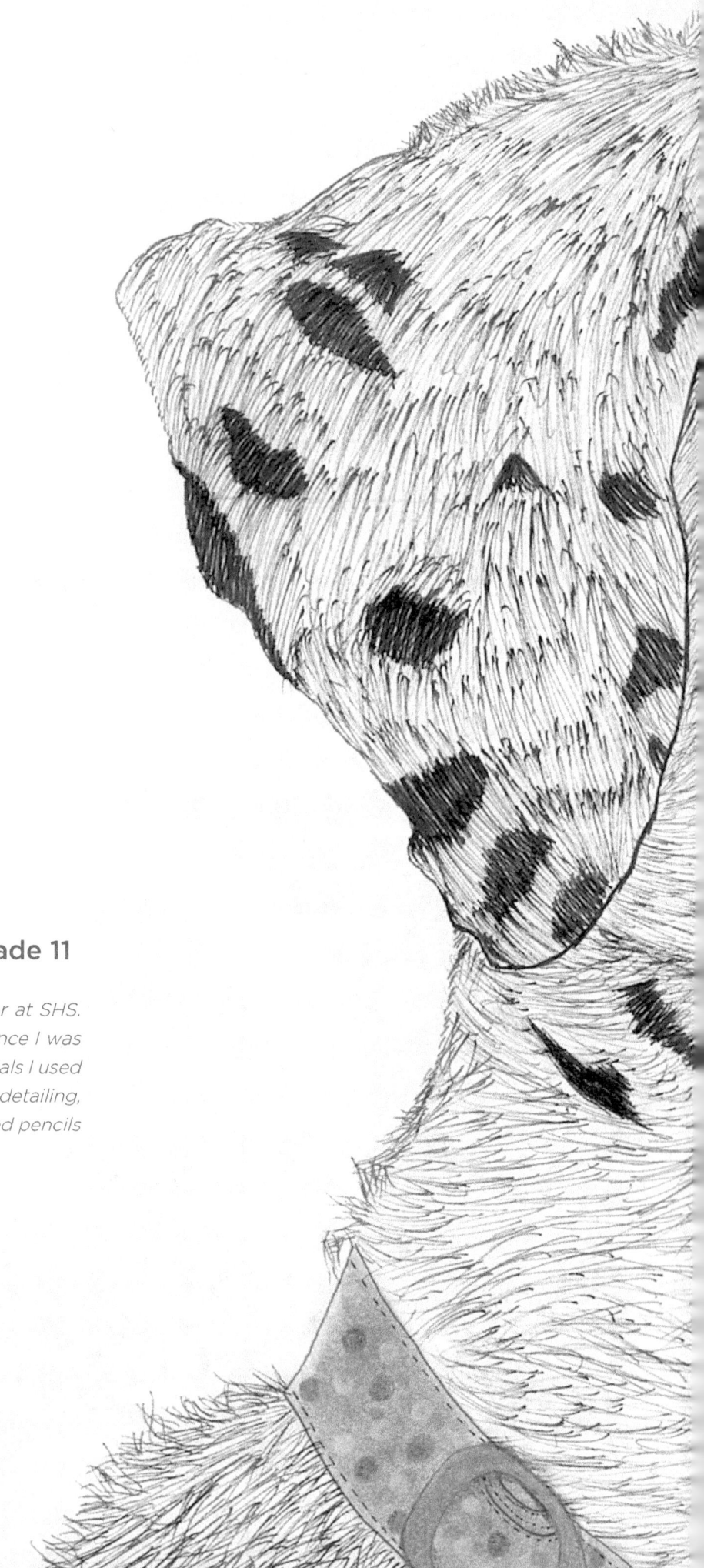

Izzy
Mixed Media | Grace Bauer, Grade 11

My name is Grace Bauer. I am 17 and a junior at SHS. I've been dancing since I was 4 and skiing since I was 2. I drew a picture of my dog, Izzy. The materials I used were pencils to lightly outline, pens for all the detailing, chalk for the eyes and collar, and lastly colored pencils for the circles on the collar.

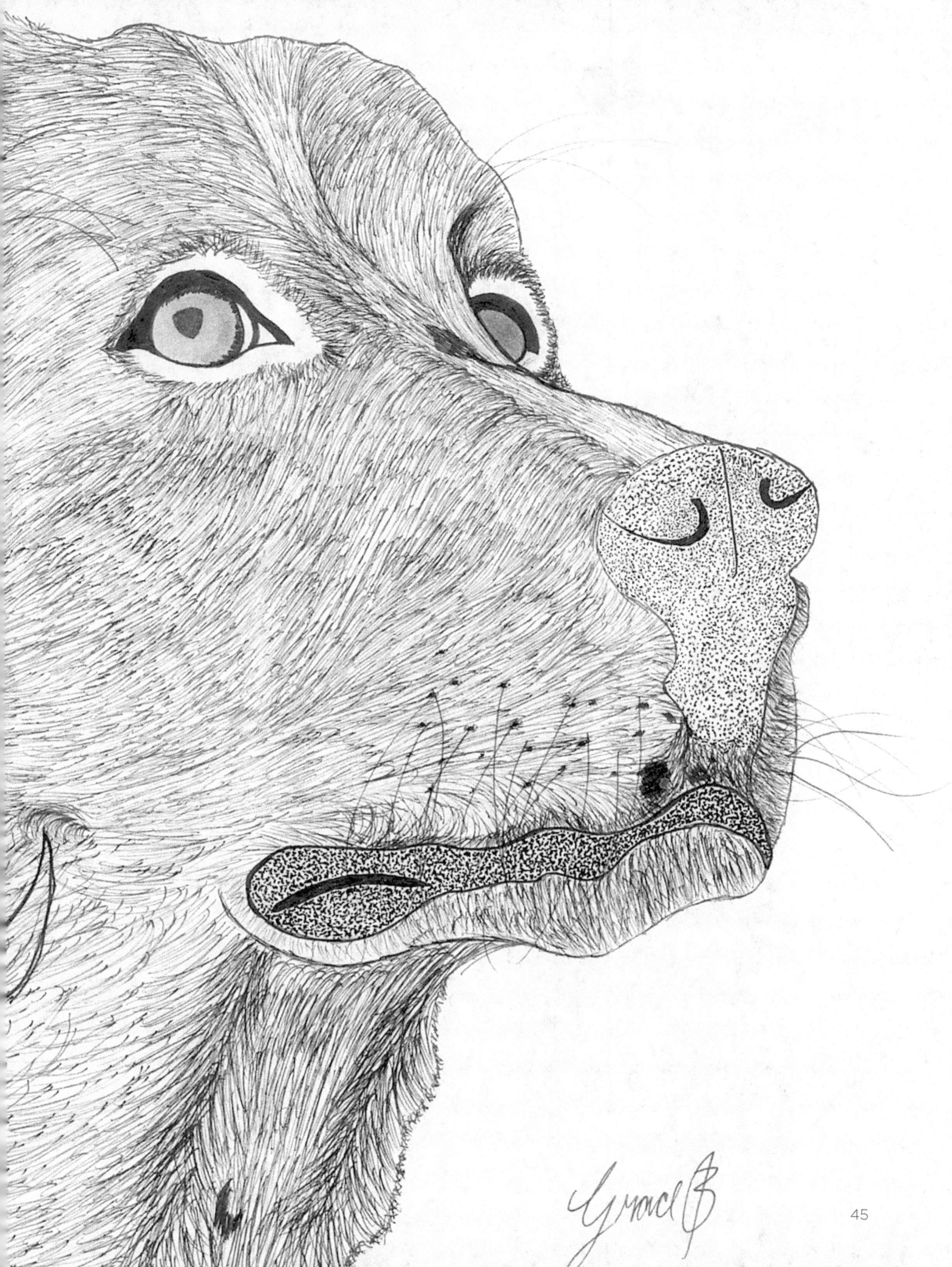

Solar System

**Mixed Media
Guadalupe Barrientos,
Grade 9**

I'm Guadalupe Barrientos, and I am a freshman at SHS. I was born in Mexico and came here when I was three months old. I had never liked drawing growing up, but when I was in middle school, all I wanted to do was draw.

One medium that I enjoy doing is drawing because I love the different options for creativity. I love making art because it is a way to cope with my stress or to keep my mind off of stuff. Like Horace said "A picture is like a poem without words."

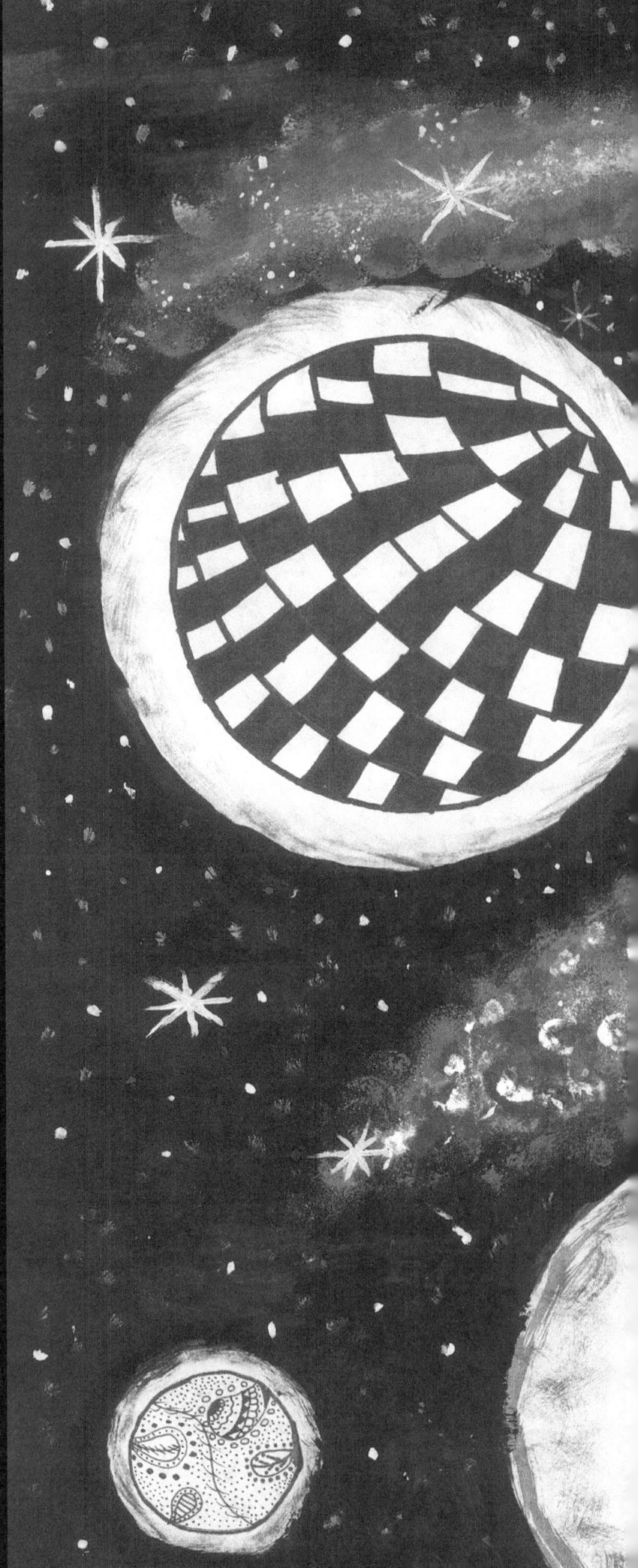

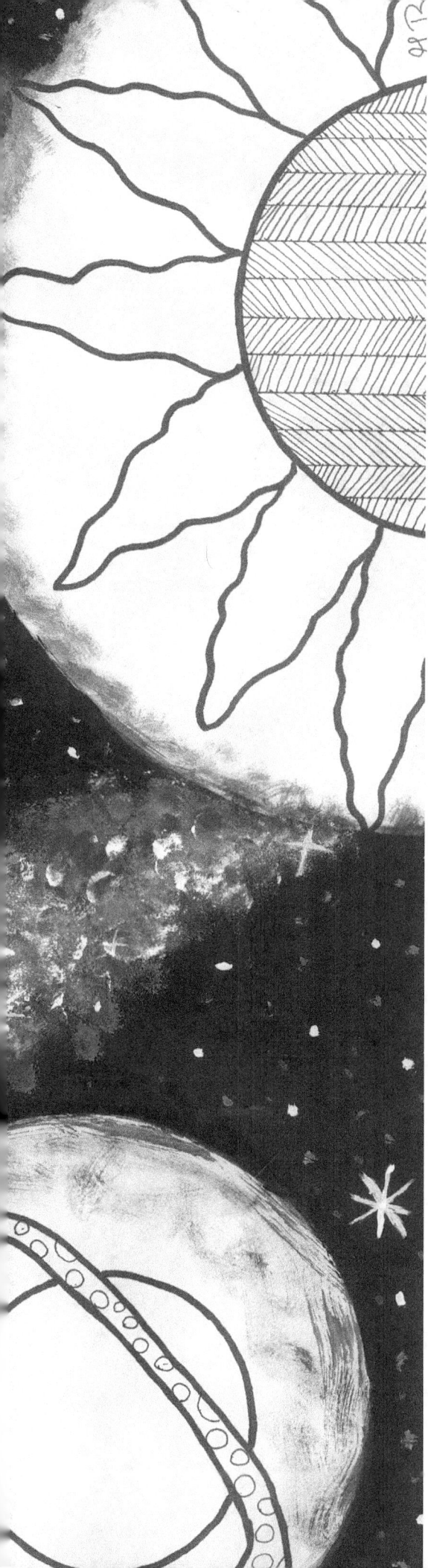

Blah Blah Blah
By Ella Eland

They speak,
The words rolling off their tongues
Like the endless tides of
The sea.
Blah, blah, blah
They crow,
Squawking out gossip
Like a flock of geese.
Their words have no depth,
No meaning
Their only purpose being
Attention.
When others sing
Of wisdom and compassion,
They cackle and screech
As if they had better voices.
Blah, blah, blah.

Quiet
By Ella Eland

I am frowned upon
For being the
Quiet
In a world that
Can't stop talking.
Quiet
They ask me why
I don't let my mouth run,
Like there is something wrong with me
For listening to them.

ABOUT THE AUTHOR *Written by Ella Eland, Author of "Labels" and "Talent" and Artist of the cover image, "Artist".*

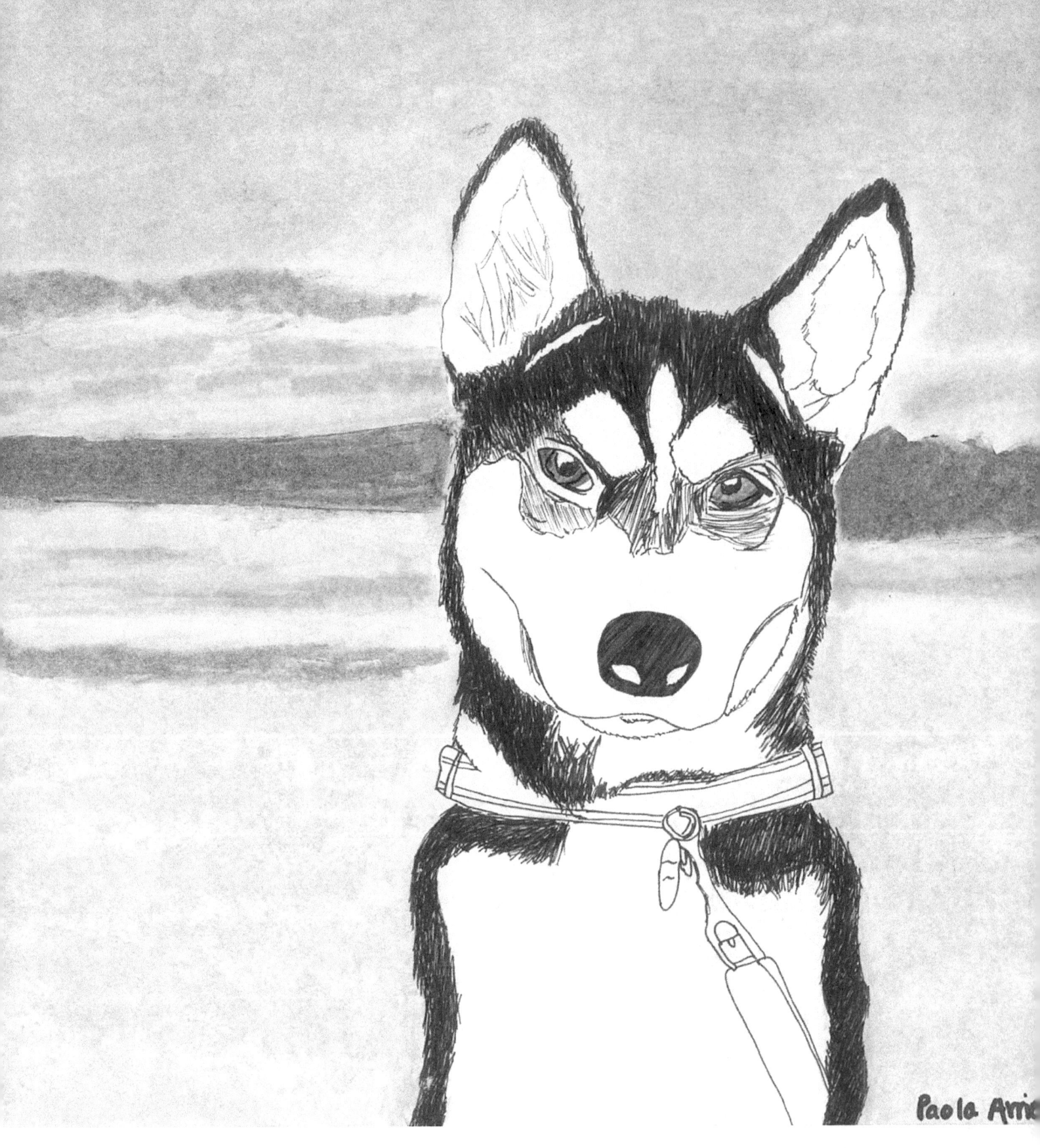

Husky

Mixed Media | Paola Arrieta, Grade 11

Learning to Ride
by Cami Davis

I had this pink bike with streamers on the handles, cool designs on the seat, all that fancy stuff. It had training wheels on it, and I was a really good rider, so I rode it a lot. I rode it to the river, I rode it when my parents went on walks, I rode it to my friends' houses. I loved that bike.

My parents alway talked about how I would be able to ride without training wheels. My dad said he could take them off and teach me how to ride without them. I didn't like this idea, but at some point, my parents decided I was ready for a bike without training wheels.

It was like learning how to ride a bike all over again, after I had already learned with the help of training wheels. My dad had to hold onto the bike seat so I wouldn't fall.

When I was ready to go, he told me, "The faster you go, the easier it is." And, since I knew that I was right, and he was wrong, I thought, "That's absurd, absolutely stupid!"

"I know it sounds weird, but it will help you balance to go faster," he informed me.

Since I had a bit of an attitude back then, I rolled my eyes, and I started to go faster, just to show him that he was wrong, and I would fall. I went faster, and faster, and, unbelievably, I actually did better when I was going faster!

Of course, I told myself that my dad was holding onto the back of my seat, so it wasn't that much of an achievement. So, I stopped, looked back, and to my astonishment, my dad was not behind me!

He didn't hold onto the seat at all, which at first made me angry at him. But then, I realized that I did it all on my own, and I was amazed. To my surprise, my dad was right, and I wasn't!

I will always remember that pink bike, and I know I can trust my parents to help me. If they are still alive by the time I get my first boyfriend, I will await their instructions.

ABOUT THE AUTHOR *My name is Cami Davis and I like riding my bike, running, and karate.*

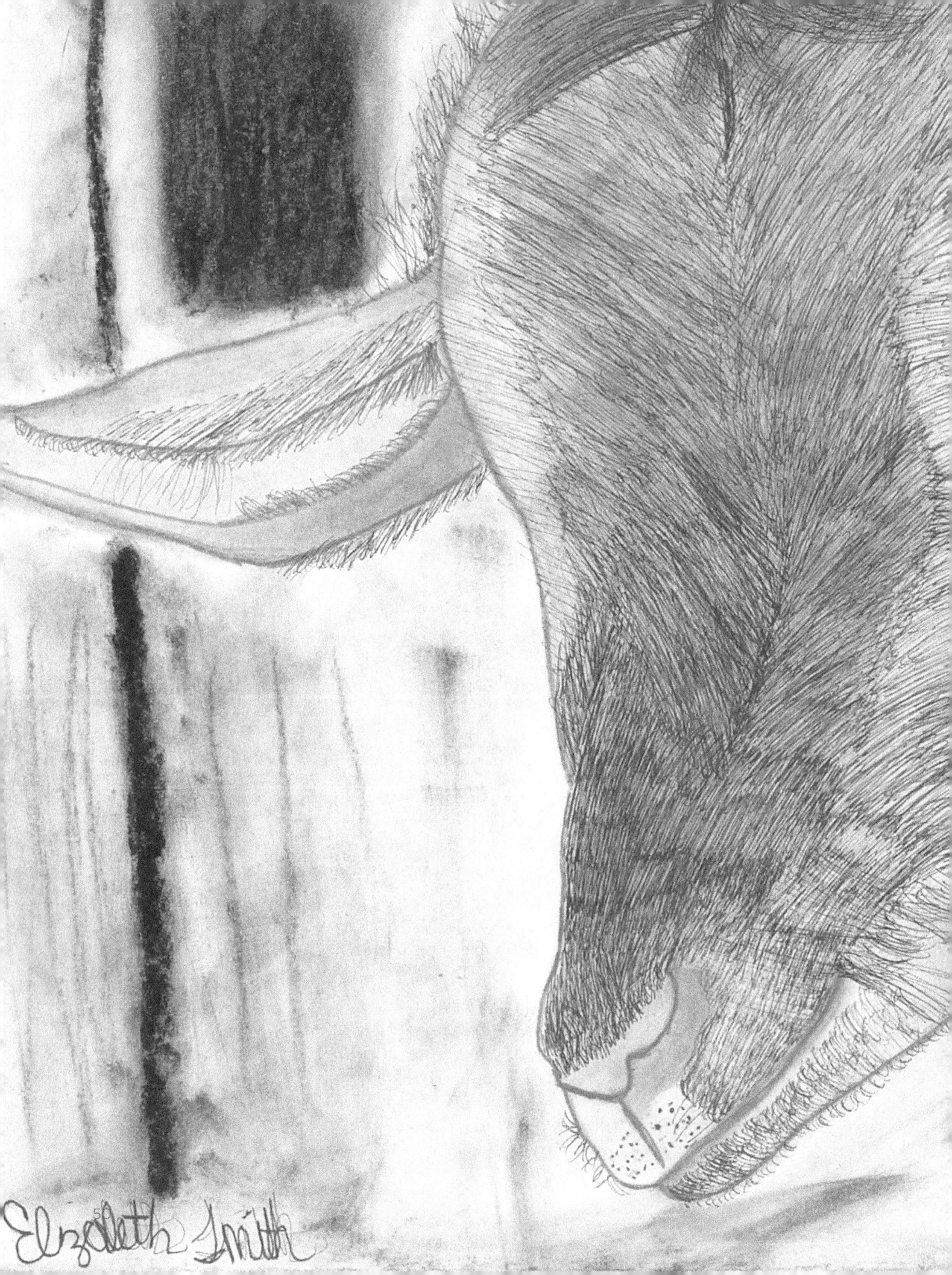

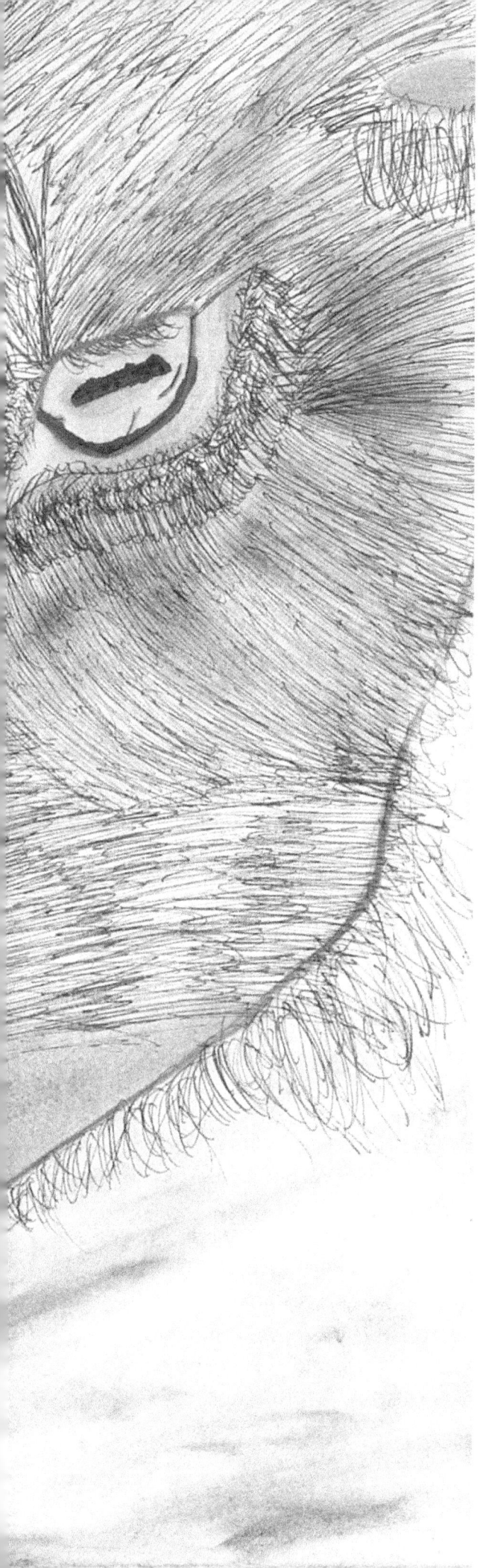

Expressive Eyes Mountain Goat

**Mixed Media
Elizabeth Smith,
Grade 10**

My version of art is drawing the thing that you see or feel when you look at a certain object or thing.

July 29

By Juniper Lee

Shiloh

There are things going through everyone's mind that they don't want anyone to know. Thoughts, memories. Secrets.

Sometimes, we don't recognize a secret when we see one. But we all know at one time or another, we will have one. It could be tiny and insignificant, or it could be the thing that alters the course of your life.

When we were little, it was a stash of candy. Then as we got older, it became a crush or a bad grade. Later on, there may be some huge secret that we are just dying to tell someone, like a weight pressing down on our shoulders that's just too heavy to carry alone.

I wanted a secret.

I needed to have something that no one knew. Something that I wanted to tell everyone but simply couldn't. A secret that was so big, it was life changing. A secret so devastatingly huge, it screamed at me to tell someone, anyone.

Unfortunately, life works in mysterious ways. I didn't know it then, but I would get exactly what I had been asking for, maybe sooner than I thought.

***

I look up, my face is soaked in tears, a bittersweet smile on my face and a bad case of nostalgia. I dab at the corners of my eyes with a tissue from a box that I now keep handy. I sigh, swallowing hard, the putrid taste of my unbrushed teeth and last night's dinner hang in my mouth. My head pounds with a migraine, and I massage my temples, the pain receding, only to come back again in waves.

I'm so confused. That had to have been the fifth time today that I've read that part of her journal, and it still doesn't seem to make any sense. We all know that she had a secret, but I seem to be the only one convinced that what happened with her was more complicated than, "your run of the mill street murder" as Chief Blakesley put it. But he's a sour person with no soul, so you can't really believe anything that he says. The idea that my aunt was killed out of pure evilness doesn't sound very reasonable to me. I tend to believe that no one can be all good or all bad--except for Chief Blakesley. I think that he's either the devil spawn or he just really really hates me for no reason in particular. It might have to do with the fact that me and his daughter have been mortal enemies since about 2 months ago.

Anyways, I'm probably getting ahead of myself. You can't understand any of what happened without the full story.

***

The first sign that my aunt was in danger was the note. It was left on our door May 5. I've burned that date into my head. My aunt's birthday. I've practiced remembering every detail of that day, over, and over again, dissecting the memory. Trying to pick out anything that I may have missed. The note was stuck to our door, wads of tape pasted on the corners as though someone was in a hurry. It was written in eerily neat handwriting, the blue ink blotched from rain earlier that day.

I came to the door first, and seeing the note excited me. I figured it must have been that boy from next door. I didn't know his name but just seeing him made my heart pound a little harder. We had walked home together a couple times and talked in school. I knew that it couldn't be for my aunt. She didn't even know anyone here, at least that's what she said. But as soon as I read the sentence, I knew, this was not meant for me,

Sorry about the note--
didn't have the time to break into your house
and leave it there.
Happy Birthday, Leela!
~ Your... friend

As soon as my aunt came up the door, she ripped the note off the door, not even bothering to read it.

"Alright, let's go inside. You can help me bake the cake." Her voice was high and strained sounding, the way it gets when she's angry and upset and maybe even scared.

But I went along with her. Smiling and nodding my head, acting as though the note didn't totally and completely freak me out. As she passed the trash can, she crumpled the note and shoved it hastily in. I'm not sure why, but I stuck my hand in after her, cringing as my fingers grazed banana peels and moldy strawberries. I found the note and stuck it into the pocket of my shorts.

From that day on, Aunt Leela always came up to the door before me. I've never seen her rip anything off the door, but I feel like there has been a feeling in the air, like something's different than before, or maybe I had just started noticing it.

***

The second sign that something was wrong were those boys. They had lined up on our front lawn at 2:00 or 3:00 on a Saturday morning, shouting and screaming at the top of their lungs. My aunt ran to wake me up, yelling nonsense about the ruckus. I couldn't tell what she was talking about, and by the time I ran out to the front of the house, they were already gone. The air reeked of chemicals from spray paint, and dripping over the newly painted house in red was, "Murderer." Aunt Leela ran out in a hastily put on green bathrobe, her tousled hair still in curlers. She just stood there and stared, her mouth slightly agape, like a fish out of water. I hardly dared to breathe.

"Inside--now." She didn't even raise her voice, but her tone dared me to question her orders. I didn't even say anything, just walked quickly inside and watched from my window as she slapped on a different shade of grey paint, not even trying to wash off the red.

Now there's just this blob of different colored paint on the side of our house. I asked her once why she never painted it over with the same shade. She just looked up from her book and said, "Our scars define us. Covering them up hides who we really are." As though it was the simplest thing.

It didn't make sense then, but every day since she died, I begin to understand everything about her more clearly. That day I thought about how we had only been in Penshaw a couple weeks, and we had already had all of this trouble. I didn't want to think about what would happen in a month, or even a year.

***

Now, the final sign came a month later. This was the last clue that something was seriously wrong. This was the scariest of all, almost more than the creepy note, the feeling, and the spray paint. It was this man. I was walking to school, my backpack swinging against my back and a smile on my face--it was Friday, and I had a class first period with a boy I liked.

I was looking down at my feet, trying not to "step on the cracks" and listening to my slightly heeled sandals click on the pavement. Thud... thud... thud. With each noise of my heels tapping the sidewalk, came another heavier stepping noise. I stopped and looked behind me, probably not wise, but it was later the thing that might have saved me.

There was a man. He was good looking and probably in his forties, with coffee-colored skin and dark hair. He smiled slightly and bobbed his head, I almost felt like I knew him from somewhere, he seemed so familiar looking. I grimaced and sped up, adjusting my backpack. Sticking my hand into the pocket of my jeans, my fingers tightly grasped a metal canister full of pepper spray. Don't ask. I think my aunt bought it for me after the boys vandalized our house, but after confronting her she, said that she had no idea what I was talking about.

I glanced back--he had sped up as well. My fingernail was under the edge of the cap, ready to flip it off and spray it. I started to jog a little and looked back at him. He wasn't running, but his pace was steadily quickening. I broke into a sprint, and he shouted at me. I couldn't quite make out what he said, but I could tell that he was aggravated.

"... your Aunt! In her... look... for the...!" but I could barely hear him, my was heart pounding too loudly in my ears.

After I lost him, I turned right around and went back to my house through the woods. I didn't even bother showing up to school. It was still another 5 minute walk there, and I didn't want him to come after me again. I ran straight home. At first my aunt was mad, but after I told her what happened, a look of fury contorted her face.

Later that night I woke up to her arguing heatedly with someone on our front porch. I peeked out my window, groggily rubbing at my sleepy eyes. It was so dark, I couldn't make out the man's face, nor tell what they were saying. My aunt shook her finger at him and stormed off, slamming the door closed. The man began walking to his car parked humming on the sidewalk.

My breath fogged up the glass, and I quickly rubbed the window clean. He paused and looked up at me, the shadows cast on his face distorted his smile and made him look like some evil creature. When I saw his face and recognized him from earlier that day, I gasped and backed up, tripping over myself on my way to bed. I lay there for hours just focusing on calming my breathing and trying to make sense of what happened.

So. There it is. Those were the signs. Unfortunately, for me--and my Aunt. I didn't do anything until it was far too late. Brushing the clues away was easy, less complicated, like ignoring a toddler nagging for my attention. Maybe I won't ever solve my aunt's murder, but, if you enjoy reading about the people of this story hopelessly struggling through my crazy life of danger and disappointment, you may just find out exactly what happened July 29, the date that my aunt, Leela Cohen, was murdered.

ABOUT THE AUTHOR *Written by Juniper Lee, author also of "The Coming".*

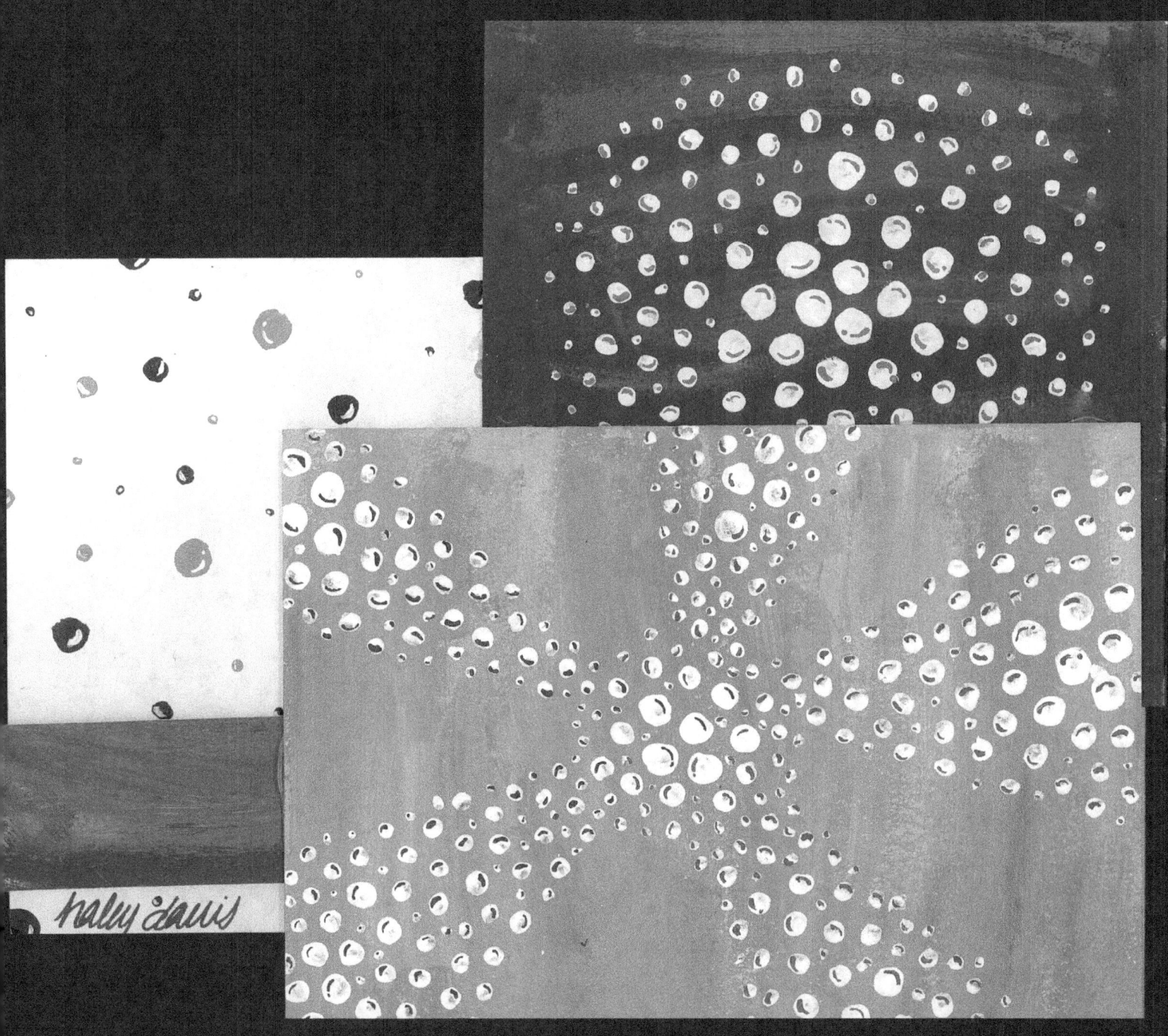

Abstract Rhythm and Pattern

Mixed Media | Haley Davis, Grade 11

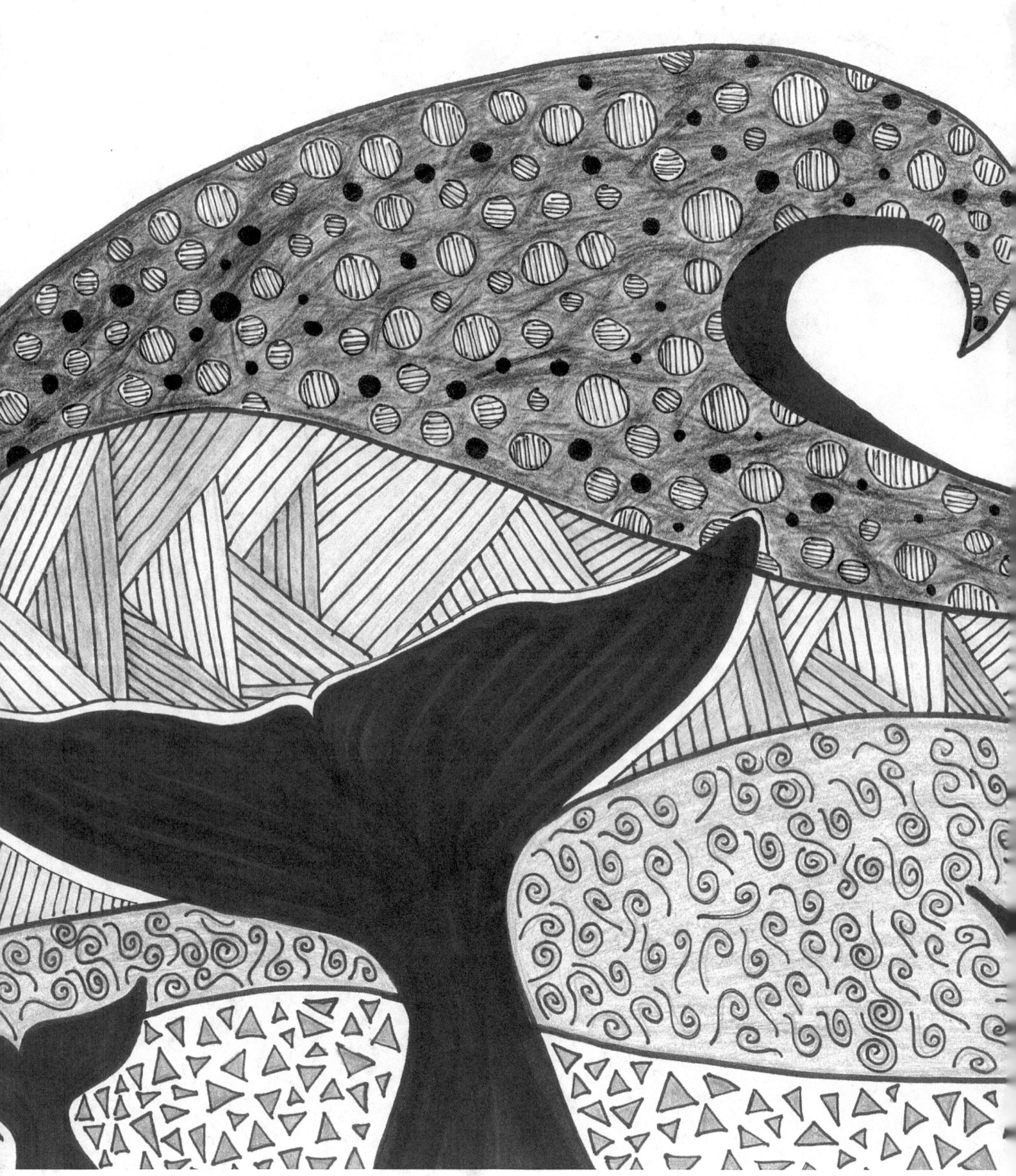

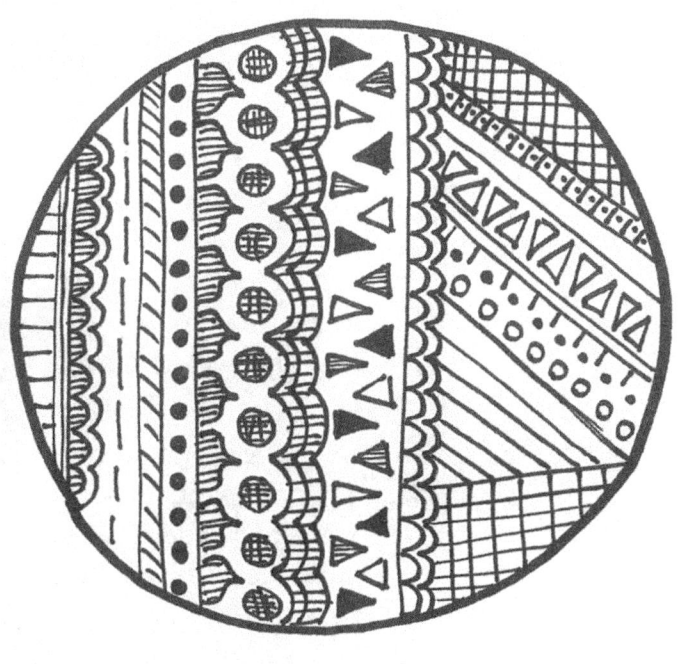

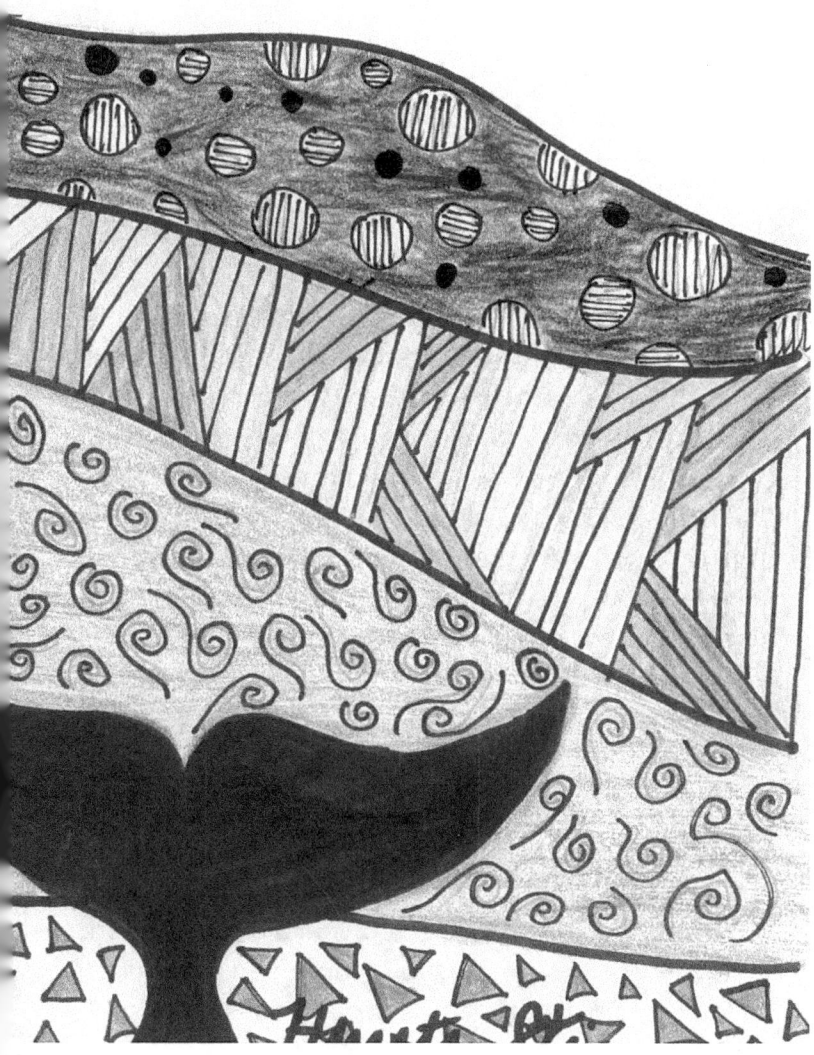

Zentangle Seascape

Pen and Ink
Hunter Stimson, 10th Grade

The purpose of art varies from person to person. For those who create art, it is a way to show expressive feelings. For those who witness the art, it is a way to understand a different point of view. For me, I create art to express ideas in my mind. I let my mind guide my hand, and allow my inner expression to come out, and I share that with my community.

Amor

By Aida Guerra

This song is in Spanish, French, and Arabic

te amo, je t'aime ', ahbak

***

Eashiqin, deux amants

"uedik alhabu walrieayat lak , wasa'uhawal fi kli wasilat litakun jadiratan habik.
sa'akun dayimaan sadiqana maeak , nawe , subur wamughfiratun.
'aeduk 'an 'uhawil 'an 'akun fi alwaqt almuhadad.
lkna al'ahamu min dhlk klh , 'ataeahid bi'an 'akun sidiyqana haqiqiaan wamukhlisana lika.
'Ahbaka."

"Prometo amarte y cuidarte,
e intentaré en todos los sentidos
ser digno de tu amor.
Siempre seré honesto contigo,
amable, paciente e indulgente.
Prometo tratar de llegar a tiempo.
Pero, sobre todo, prometo ser un verdadero
y leal amigo para ti.
Te amo."

"aeudk 'an takun habibik, rafiqik wasadiquk,
sharik hayatik fi al'ubuat,
halifik fi alsirae,
'akbar maejib bik wa'aseab khasm ladik.
rafiquk fi almughamarat,
altaalib walmuelim alkhasu bik,
eaza'ak fi khaybat al'amal,
sharikik fi al'adhaa.
hadha hu nadhr muqadas lakum ya mutasaw fi kli shay'in. kla shay'an."

"Prometo ser tu amante, compañero y amigo,
Tu compañero en la paternidad,
Tu aliado en conflicto,
Tu mejor fan y tu adversario más duro.
Tu camarada en aventura,
Su estudiante y su maestro,
Tu consuelo en decepción,
Tu cómplice en travesuras.
Este es mi voto sagrado para ti, mi igual en todas las cosas. Todas las cosas."

"I Love You"

Love (translation)

I love you, I love you, I love you,

Two lovers, Two lovers

"I promise to love and care for you,
and I will try in every way to be worthy of your love.
I will always be honest with you, kind, patient and forgiving.
I promise to try to be on time.
But most of all, I promise to be a true and loyal friend to you.
I love you."

Repeat in Spanish

"I promise to be your lover, companion and friend,
Your partner in parenthood,
Your ally in conflict,
Your greatest fan and your toughest adversary.
Your comrade in adventure,
Your student and your teacher,
Your consolation in disappointment,
Your accomplice in mischief.
This is my sacred vow to you, my equal in all things. All things."

Repeat in Spanish

"I Love You"

ABOUT THE AUTHOR
My name is Aida Guerra, and I live in Frisco, Colorado. I am in 6th grade at Summit Middle School.

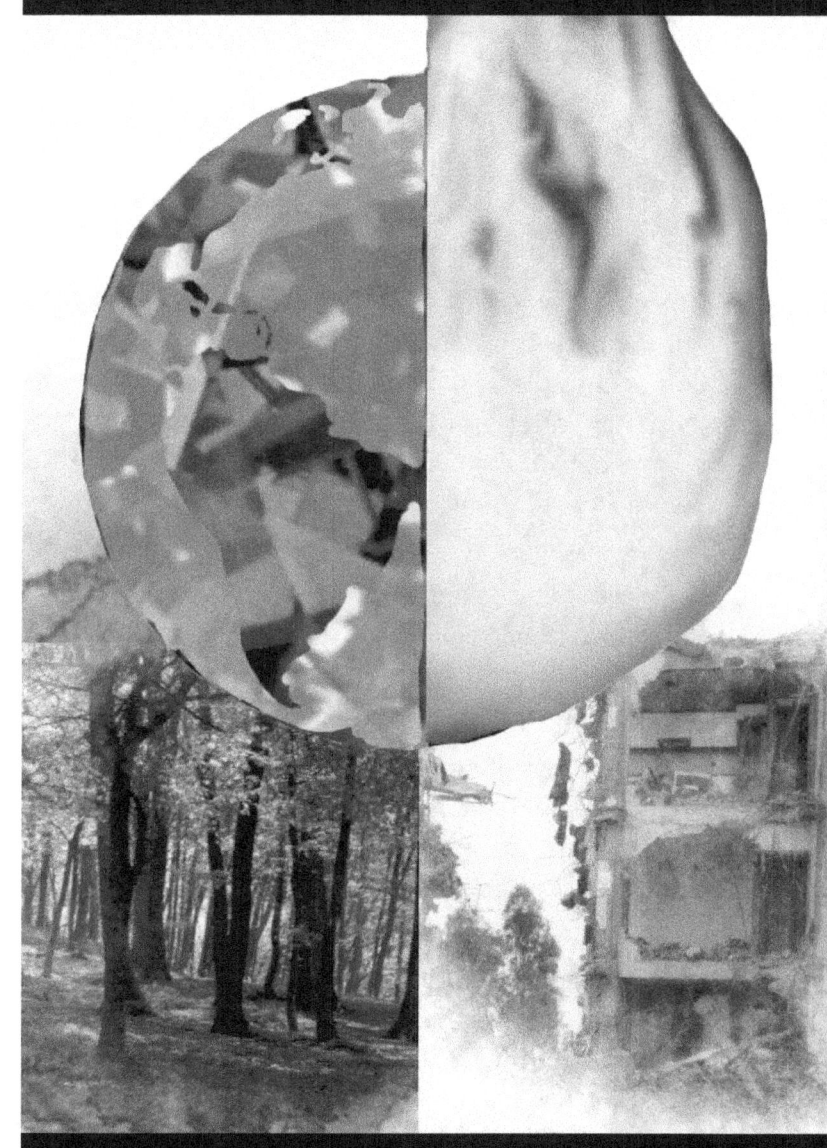

World Split in Two

Digital Media
Julia Horvath, Grade 8

I'm Julia Horvath, an 8th grade student in Summit Middle School. I am a ski racer for Team Breckenridge Sports Club, and I have been racing for 6 years. I found a few years ago that I have an interest in art, and started painting. I started with acrylics and just recently tried oil paints for the first time. For this piece of art I, gave digital online art a try to see how it would go, and I found that I really like it.

Crash

By Nascha Martinez

Ch. 1 - Plane

Today we were going to visit my good-for-nothing brother, Ian in San Diego. I will never be able to guess why my parents wanted to visit him; after all, he left us when we needed him most. Once my parents' stupid fighting got worse, he left, which resulted in my parents' divorce.

"Amelia, get packed. I don't care what you think of your brother. He invited us over. It's a big deal to spend time with family. He is still family," my mother called.

"I do not care if he is family; he left us when we needed him most. I don't know why you are making me go," I yelled, slamming my door so I could no longer hear my mother.

When I was done packing, I headed to the car and shut the door. I felt like crying then but managed to hold it in. I hadn't cried since my parents got their divorce, and I didn't want to now.

My mom hopped into the car and started the engine. I sighed; I wish things were the way they used to be…my parents were happy, and so was I.

I fell asleep. It was one of those sleeps where you are swimming in black--thick, gooey black, and when I woke up, we were at the airport.

"Jessie,…erm…we are here. I know this might be a little strange going on this trip with me, but I am sure we can manage," my mother called to my father.

"I know, DJ, but can we discuss this somewhere else?" my father said, giving my mom "a look."

She nodded, and we headed for security. After that, we headed for the airplane and got there right as it was about to take off. Sadly, it looked like we were going to get to see my brother.

Ch. 2 - The Crash

"Beep, beep, beep," sirens went off inside the plane. I saw air whizz past my window. We were crashing.

"Amie, unbuckle!" my mom screamed

"What?!" I shouted back.

"Just do it. If we crash, you might be able to get out of the plane faster. Ok?" She tried to speak normally, but I could hear the fear in her voice. I unbuckled.

"BOOM!" the plane exploded from impact.

I was sent flying, and a rock hit my head. Then everything went black.

When I woke up, there was a painful ache in my head, but it was not too bad, and I was able to stand up just fine. I could also remember everything that had just happened, so I figured I had not gotten a concussion. I think I passed out mainly from fear, so I think the rock just scared me even more.

I was in a vast desert. Cacti towered at least a foot above my head; its needles were towering at odd angles.

"Jessie? DJ?…Mom? Dad? Are you guys there?" I called. No one replied. I began to cry. The tears were hot, and I couldn't see through them. I sat down. They came in such big waves that it felt as if a tsunami was coming from my eyes. I had not cried in so long that it felt odd, almost painful. I must have cried for about an hour because when I was done, the first rays of dawn were coming in.

After my slightly annoying cry, I began to think straight. The light is beginning to come through these dark clouds, so it is near morning… Good!

I will be able a lot see a lot better.

Ok, I am stranded in the Nevada desert with a week's amount of food and an empty water bottle. I also have nowhere to sleep, and there are many venomous rattlesnakes and maybe scorpions. There is probably a town some miles from here. There should be someone there who can help me. Ok, I should get going.

Ch. 3 - Rain

I trudged on for many miles, but my stomach began to rumble, and I stopped to eat. At least I had my backpack. I was relieved to find it still intact. I gulped down some pomegranate seeds and a slice of bread from my bag, and I looked around for something to drink.

Suddenly my wish was granted. Rain began to fall, and I collected all the water in my water bottle that my mom had made me bring on the plane for "safety" reasons, and caught at least a little more in my mouth. Now I had a one-to-two-day supply of water, and my main issue was somewhere to sleep.

Aha, there was a large rock that could shelter me and the blanket I brought on the plane. I climbed up the rock and made a roost and fell asleep. My dreams were nice and comforting. I dreamed that my family was the way it used to be, and the plane trip to San Diego was just a little vacation trip, and we had the best time there.

I woke up to more rain. My blanket was soaked. Ugh, now I was really cold. I had been really hot. I didn't know which was worse.

I started on my long journey again. I was pretty sure I was at least six miles away from the plane. I had been walking long enough.

Ch. 4 - Prints

I had been counting the days as I walked, hoping for a rescue. All my water was gone, and all I had left of the food was bread. There was no rescue as far as I could see. I was 20 miles away from the plane.

Stupid search and rescue, stupid brother, stupid world, stupid life.

I didn't care what happened. I just wanted to go home.

Suddenly, I saw something. A track, a thin line in the ground was following some prints that looked almost human-like. I figured the person must have been dragging some cloth on the ground, and it made a print.

I thought there must be a town nearby. I ran, following the tracks. They led in many different directions, and all of them were the same prints, so I figured the person must have taken a lot of wrong turns.

I also noticed a very, very large black scorpion coming towards me. I screamed and ran for my life, still following the tracks. It came after me. I could almost feel the venom going through my body. I had never run so fast in my entire life. Almost everything was blurry except the prints.

After what seemed like days, the scorpion stopped chasing me, and I caught my breath.

I was standing on top of one of the human-like prints, and I felt relieved to know that I had been following the track.

"Hiss, hissssss," the noise was quiet, but still audible. I turned around in all directions, but didn't see anything.

"Hisss," I figured it was the wind, but the noise still scared me and I kept walking.

Every time I turned around the noise stopped; it all was making me very on edge.

Ch. 5 - Venom

I was too tired to go any further, and I stopped for a rest. I thought the hissing noise was probably just in my head, so I lay down on a rock and fell asleep.

"Owwwwwww!" I screamed.

I had been bitten. A rattlesnake was slithering

away from me, and my foot burned very painfully. It was even beginning to swell. My foot was getting bigger by the minute. I ran as hard as I could, but it hurt far too badly to continue.

All the day's worries suddenly hit me, and I fell to the ground too tired and sad to go on. Maybe this was all a nightmare. Gosh, I thought, and fell back into a deep sleep.

Ch. 6 - Oh, Brother

"I... what are you doing here? Where am I?" I said.

"Hi, Amelia!" someone called from the doorway.

"Who are you?"

"Hi... I am your brother. Owww!" he yelled, as he tried to get through the door but hit his head on the ceiling.

"You!" I said with a tightness in my tone.

He brushed a strand of dark hair out of his eyes. "Amelia, are you okay? You look so much older, I can barely recognize you," he said.

I snorted. "I bet you wouldn't." A pain shot through my leg, and I winced. Looking down I saw a tiny moon-shaped scar curving up from my foot.

"Amelia... I...," he shook his head. "Does it hurt? Please... you were out there for weeks..." he faltered, his eyes misting up.

I couldn't help it; my voice softened a little. "What do you think?!"

"I'm sure it does. Don't worry. You will be able to walk again in about a week. Dad, erm, passed on. Mom will be coming to see you. She suffered a broken leg and fractured her wrist, but... nothing more. Search and rescue found her a week before you."

"Mom," I gasped as she came over to me, sobbing and hugging me tightly to her chest.

"Oh my gosh. Oh, Amelia! Thank my lucky stars you are alright. Oh!"

She grasped me so tightly that I couldn't breath, and Ian had to pull her off of me.

"Mom, how did our plane crash? What happened?" I asked, regaining my breath.

"Well, the pilot had a heart attack and lost control. The co-pilot tried to pull up, but we were too near the ground. He told the airport we were fine and that he could get us to safety. But he thought wrong."

I nodded and fell back into a deep sleep.

Ch. 7 - Home

We went home the next day with an airport supplied jet. When we arrived, we found a big crowd waiting for us, and they gave us flowers and candy. I never thought this many people would be waiting for us! After thanking them profusely, we finally arrived at our house.

My brother came to live with us. I couldn't believe it. We were all back in New York. We were finally home.

ABOUT THE AUTHOR *Hi, my name is Nascha Martinez. I am 10 years old and in the 5th grade. Some of my hobbies are swimming, skiing, and reading.*

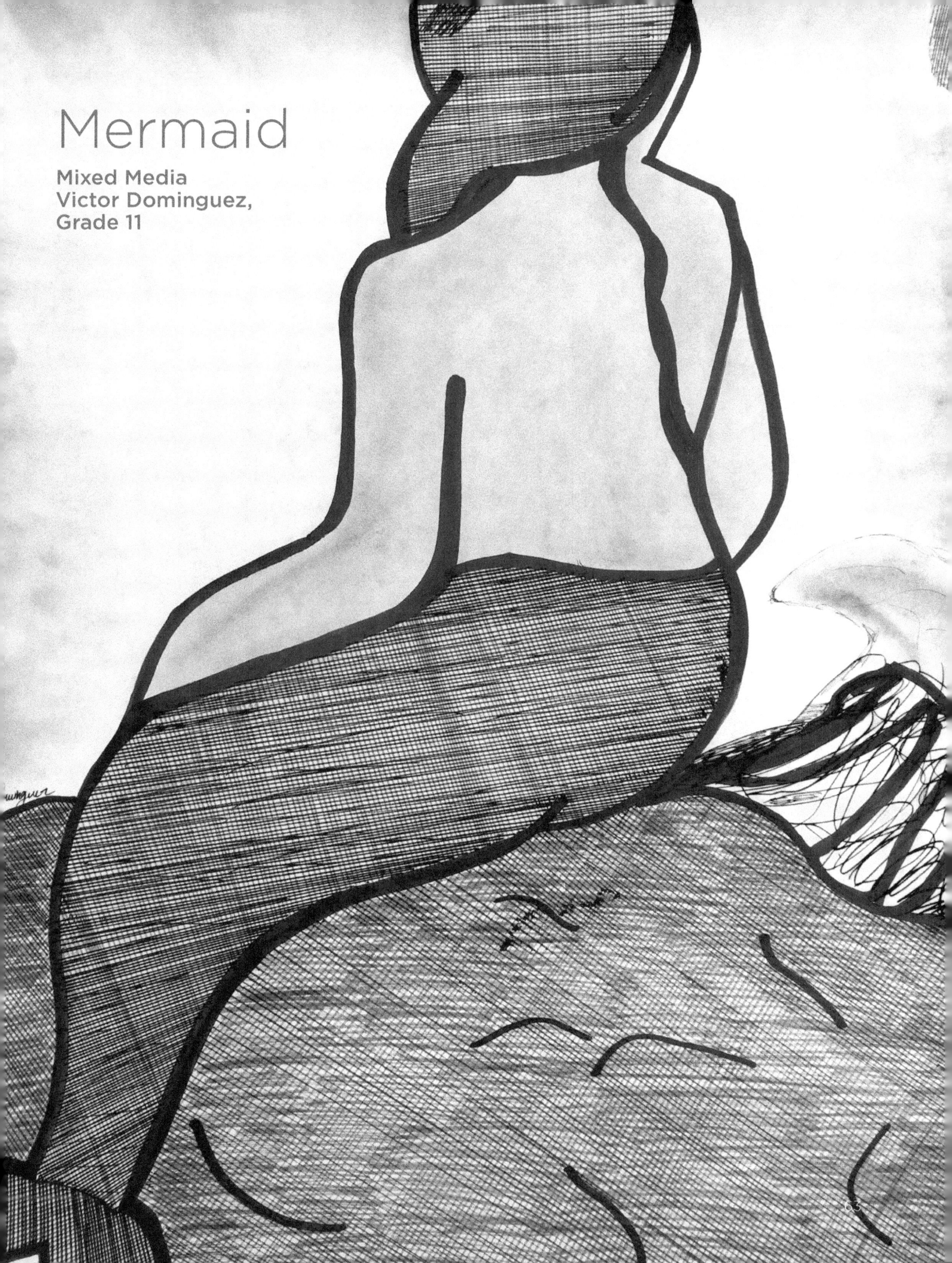

Mermaid

Mixed Media
Victor Dominguez,
Grade 11

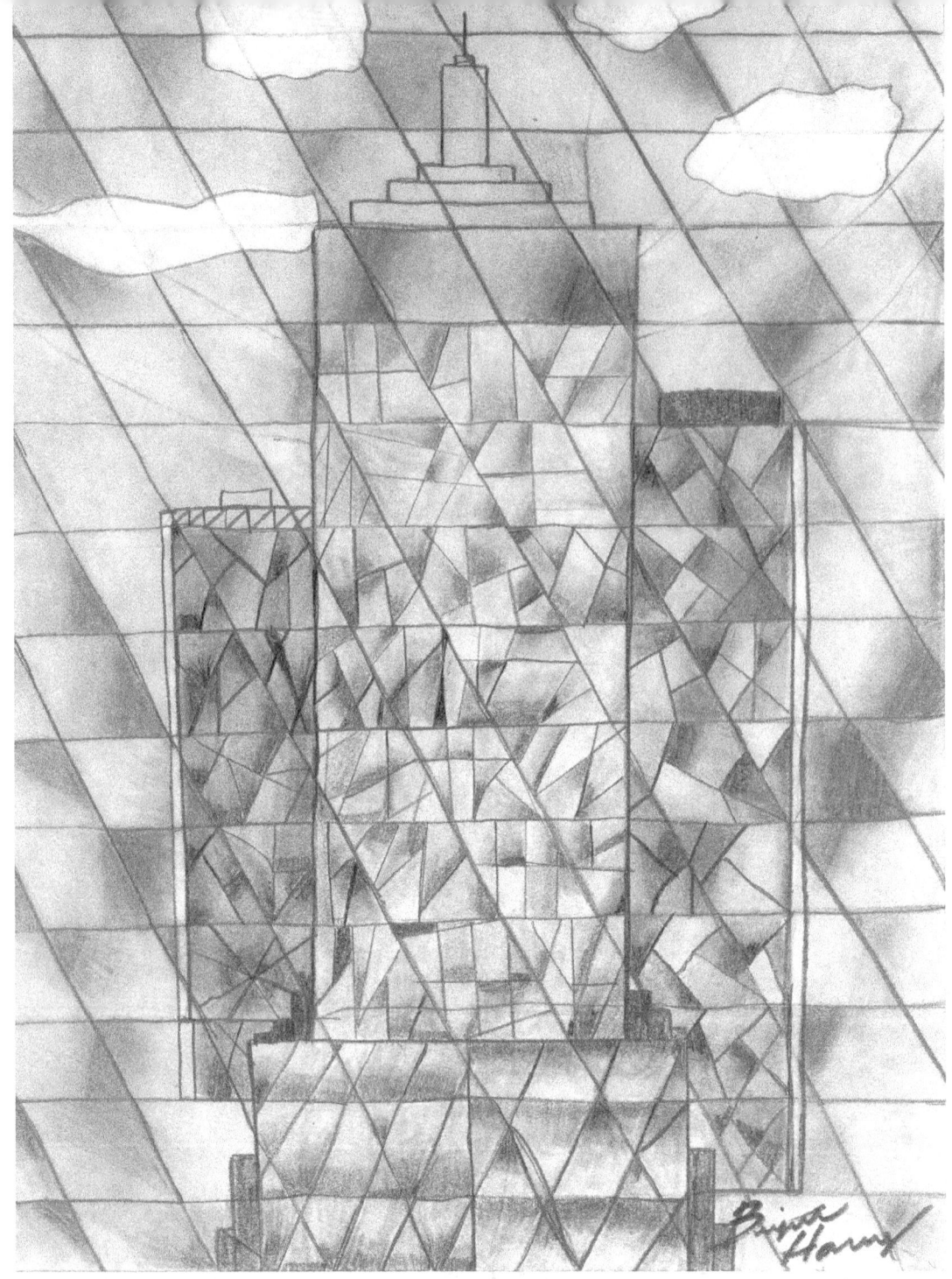

Shattered Value Cityscape

Graphite | Bridgette Hough, Grade 10

I love art because you can express yourself through your work. It makes you think about things, and it can make you feel. It is a peaceful activity that calms the mind. I love drawing. Any type of art, even though drawing is hard, is a pastime. My creative process starts with an idea. Then I begin to sketch it out. I keep adding more as my mind sees it. I try to use good composition. The meaning of my art is to keep myself creating and learning. Art helps the world see culture and the different minds of the world. Art should be carried on through generations and never stop.

You are nicer than a croissant is tasty
You are funnier than Grumpy Cat is well, grumpy

I like walking with you,
kind of like a toddler likes mac n' cheese

The last reason I have is that you are imaginative,
like a penguin that can fly.

ABOUT THE AUTHOR *My name is Cooper McMullen, and I live in the mountains of Colorado. I love the outdoors and animals so much that one of my best friends is my dog. My favorite book is <u>The Mark of Athena</u> by Rick Riordan, but I love all books about mythology. I have a little brother who loves my stories a lot, so I hope you enjoy them as much as he does.*

Hunted by Swords
By Peri Habermas

Orean

"Millennia ago we lived as one with our neighbors. We were known to live among each other, to share our cultures with each other. We were one with each other, yet greed and hate led to the separation of our races. The humans became hungry for power and gold; with hearts of stone they stole, murdered, and burned until only one remained." With open eyes and frightened faces the children watched as the young woman continued her story.

"To prevent the corruption of the remainder of the world, a barrier would be built, not of stone, but of air. The greatest minds of the century united to create a formula that would change the properties of the air on one side of the world. A controlled gas was then spread into every house, street, and person with a good heart to change their lung cells. But the chemical did something unexpected; it evolved the people to become a different race, one that was stronger, smarter, and more powerful than the humans.

"We are these changed beings. We are known as the Alteration. In a way we symbolize the practice of kindness and generosity, while they symbolize all things unforgiving and merciless. It was because of the darkness in the humans' hearts that they remain virtually powerless, and we use the power that is ours to create harmony and peace within our lands. God forbid what would happen if the humans learned what power we wielded. And so we continue to---"

A voice full of alarm shouted for her attention. As Orean looked up, the messenger slowly said, "Our leader is missing."

"I know," Orean quietly said, "I was there when he went through the barrier."

"The barrier! How...when...why?"

Suddenly, all the pain and anger of the past few days exploded from inside her, "You know perfectly why, Messenger; our world is dying. With each passing minute we do nothing, our world is turning black, being drained of its power, and we don't know how!" As her brief spurt of anger passed, she walked out of the door and departed. Finally free of the confinement of the school room, Orean ran and ran until her clan had disappeared beyond the mountains.

A sob shuttered through her body as she wept, and with sudden clearness she recalled the last thing her leader had said to her, "Alone we are an experiment. Alone we are a disease. But together we are the Alteration. Together, we are one with nature, with each other, and our world. This is what you tell yourself if you ever feel in doubt of who you are. Always know that we are here to support you, in life or death."

With these final words Orean's leader and friend walked through the barrier and disappeared into the simmering light.

Now, turning around, Orean was preparing for the run home when a pulse of magic shuddered through her; someone had entered the barrier.

Orean knew that every being in Doerwald had felt the pulse of magic. It was as if the barrier was warning them, speaking to them about an unwanted life form in their world. As if on instinct, she followed the pulse. She used the magic to guide her feet to the source.

A current of white hot magic swept through her causing her to shudder, she was close.

Keres

Running for his life, Keres dodged trees and rocks, yet nothing seemed to cease the guard's pace. Then he reached it. The barrier, the only thing that separated Othslam from the oasis of Doerwald. Looking at it, the rebel stopped. The Alterations in Doerwald was the only thing that could save his world from the king who ruled over the humans with an iron fist.

He had to relay the message to these people. He had to get their help, or there would be no hope.

"There he is! Get him!" The guards were gaining on him.

"This is it," Keres mumbled to himself as he leapt into the world that would decide his fate.

A flash of light, and he was through. He had finally made it. He, the rebel, the traitor, and now perhaps, the savior. Yet, in his flee from the capital city of Morlyn, Keres forgot that he couldn't breathe the new atmosphere. The freedom fighters he joined had a small supply of air masks. The masks would supply oxygen, should he choose to travel to the other side. In his haste Keres had no time to grab one from headquarters without exposing the location of the freedom fighters. His breath shaking, Keres suddenly became disoriented. Slowly swaying, he began to lose consciousness.

But before he did, a beautiful woman of gray entered his vision. The last thing he saw were those beautiful white eyes staring down at him.

Orean and Keres

Keres woke in a room full of gray people dressed in silver.

"What is going on?" he asked, "Where am I?"

Gesturing to the room Orean stated, "You are in the council of the elders. I am Orean, and here you will tell your story and make your offer."

Briefly, Keres told them his name and why he was here and why he needed their help. He told them of the corruption of power in Othalam and how the king was using this world to power his. Still, even after he explained, they looked skeptical. They whispered amongst themselves, eyeing him suspiciously. Keres's patience began to wear thin, and he soon became frustrated that they still wouldn't listen.

"He is stealing your power," Keres yelled, "Don't you understand? He is using your power to provide for his army. It is giving our dictator the power he needs to rule the world."

Calmly the clan leader said to the fighter, "We care not what your dictator does to your side of this earth. We only care to rid our side of the blackness you humans have placed there."

"If you want Doerwald to heal, you must help me free Othalam from the king's grasp." Keres glanced pleadingly at Orean. Without her voice in the matter, he would never get the people of this land to support him.

Looking into the pleading eyes of Keres, Orean saw not a man who betrayed his country, but instead she saw a man that would do anything to save it.

Breaking her contact with Keres, Orean stood and addressed the court, "I will leave with him. This may be the only way to save our land, our people. I will not stand by as our people get swallowed up by this darkness."

"You, you are right, Orean," the clan leader said quietly. "Our people don't deserve this." Turning toward Keres he asked, "How do we stop this?"

The Barrier

They prepared to leave. Away from the room full of the clan, Orean questioned Keres, "How are we going to manage to sneak into the castle and disconnect the main power line of magic from the throne? There has to be security everywhere protecting this connection between our world and the throne."

"It is not impossible. All we must do is break the throne, and everything should be placed back in order," he replied. Moving steadily toward the shimmering barrier in front of them, Keres turned to Orean and asked, "Shall we begin?"

Together, they disappeared into the light.

ABOUT THE AUTHOR *My name is Peri Habermas, and I am in the eighth grade at Summit Middle School. I have a strong passion for music and currently play the violin and piano, but just recently I have discovered my love for writing. I began writing this year on an online software, and I have fallen in love with it ever since.*

Shattered Value Carnations

**Graphite
Soledad Borrego,
Grade 10**

My name is Soledad, and I am a Sophomore. I am very passionate about the arts: theater, fashion and drawing. I chose to draw carnations as they have many layers, and I wanted them to be more acknowledged. I love making art, as it brings out creativity and enjoyment. I find that most people work hard on art, as it shows who they are and their interests, and I think this is a very pleasant idea. My work is about what is honest, expressive and spiritual. For me, I think that each creation of art I have represents a deeper meaning. The carnations were united together. The outer layers embraced the darker values, and the lighter layers bring out the brightness.

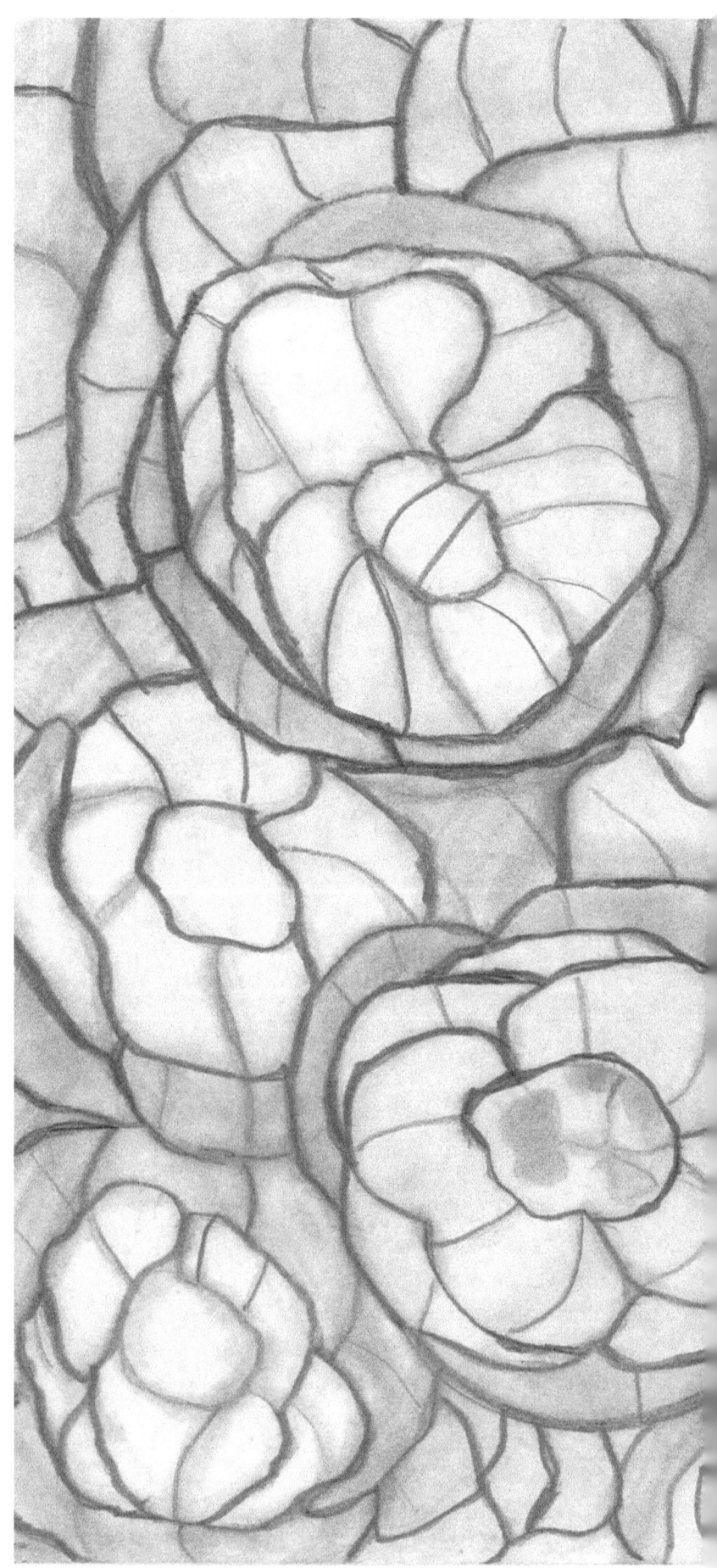

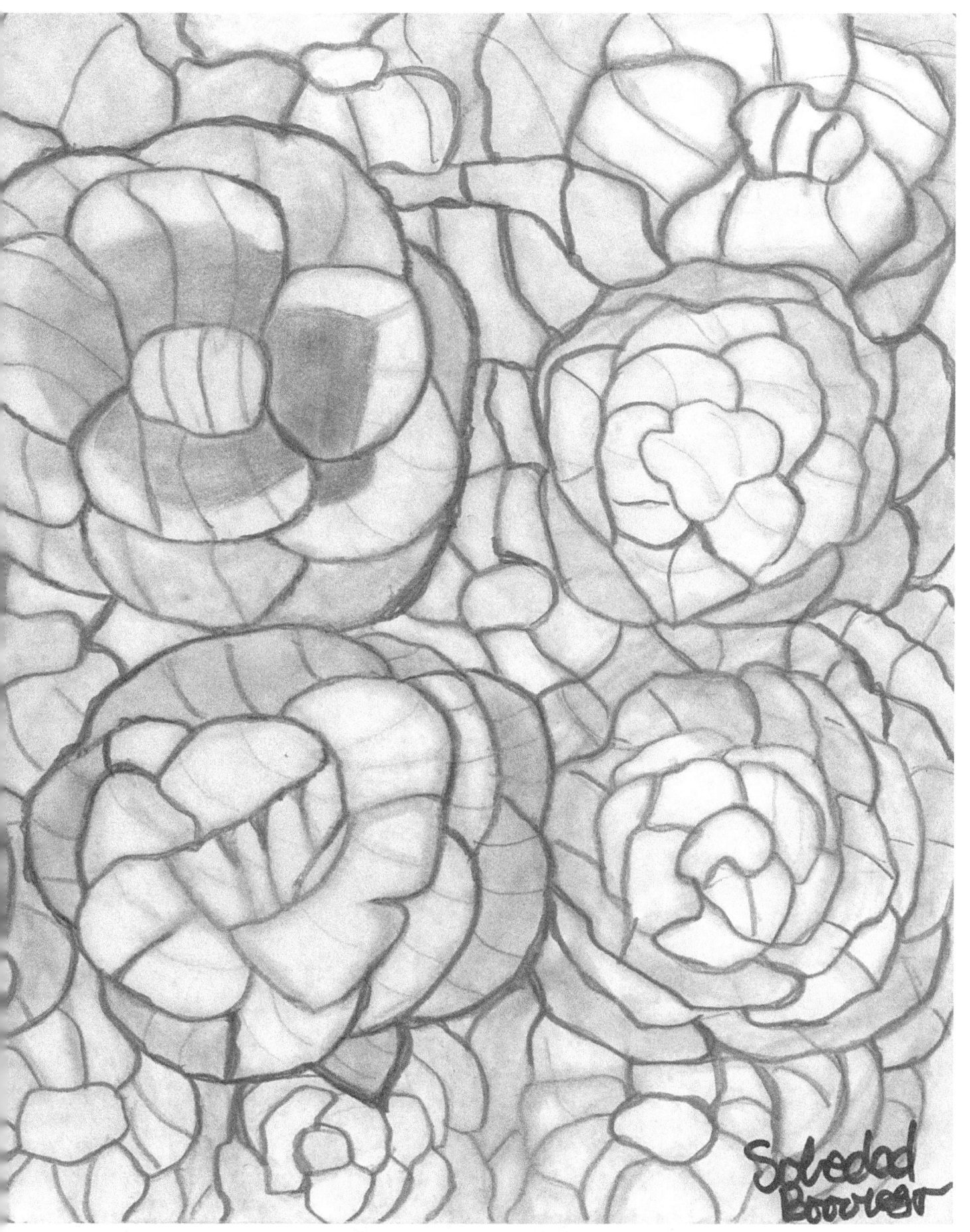

Ranch Horse
Ink | Miguel Gomez, Grade 10

I am a Sophomore at Summit High School. I like riding horses, and I enjoy being active. I hope to own a ranch one day.

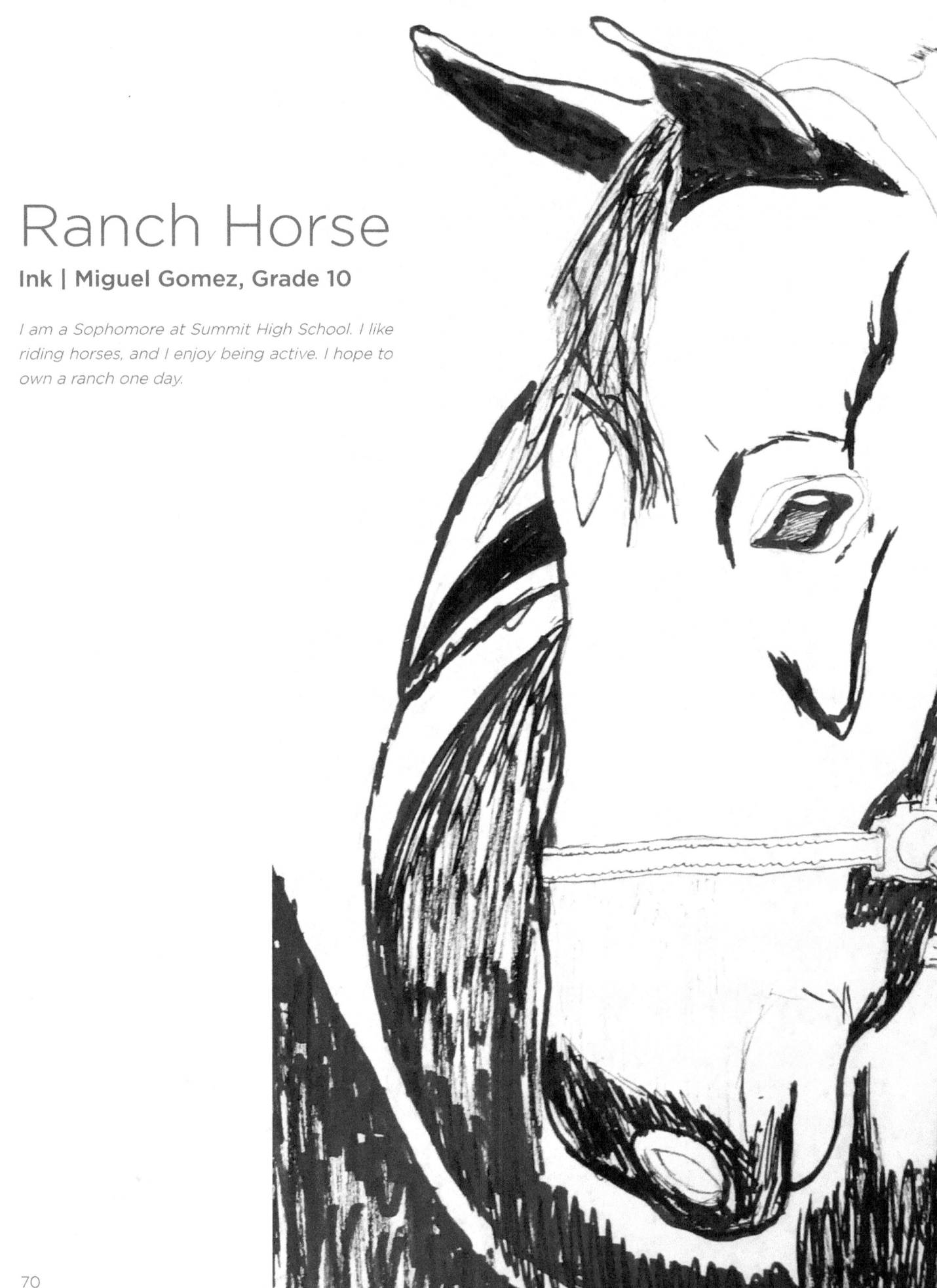

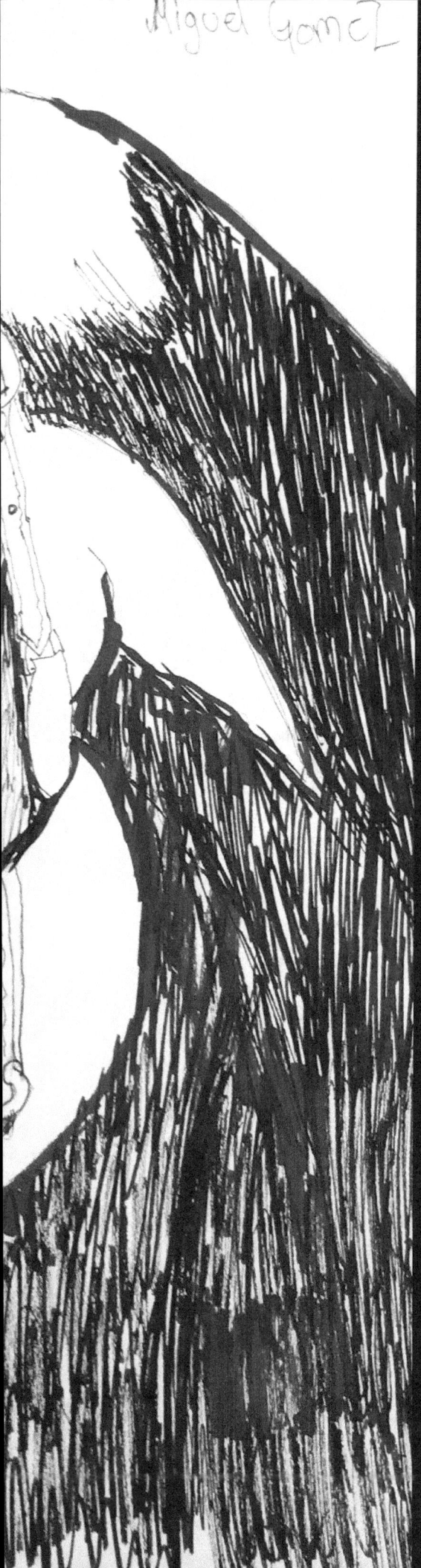

Nature in Winter
by Luke Klasnick

The snow is white and falling,
The tree stands strong,
Mountains are calling,
While they sing their happy song.

A river's water flowing,
Under the icy cold,
The trail's beauty showing,
How nature is so bold.

ABOUT THE AUTHOR
I am 10 years old and have lived in Breckenridge for the past two years. Skiing is my favorite activity. There is nothing better than being outside, which is what inspired me to write this poem. This poem is using the writing style of Robert Louis Stevenson. I hope you like it.

Saving The Titanic
By Mary Grace Butler

"Mum, are you sure that I won't miss that much school?" I asked.

"No, Alizah! We are just taking a short trip to the United States on the Titanic."

"Ugh, who cares about homework and school? You are such a nerd. I just want to see an actual RMS ship." This was my older adopted brother, Collin.

You see, I never asked for a brother, and I never needed a brother. It was just me and my dolls. But, this brother was always teasing me about these things. Collin had been raised working on a farm and basically never going to school. We had adopted him in the first place because he had gotten into some type of trouble with the government. After that, he was sent to a rehab school in France. There, he did all sorts of things. You know, working in the community, stuff like that. My father, who had represented the estate was contacted when they decided that that wasn't a good fit for Collin. They had decided to adopt him because, they thought that, quote on quote, I needed to have someone around the house. Honestly, I am not five, but, of course I just said, "Okay,".

So, off my parents went, making arrangements and finally, BOOM, I had a new older brother. I mean he wasn't a bad person. He would take me places and play with me sometimes. But I had a feeling that he didn't really want to. I just hated when he'd tease me. I still loved him and couldn't remember what it was like without him. But it hurt when he teased me. Honestly, I don't think he cares. Or maybe he doesn't know.

At that moment, my train of thought was interrupted due to my father walking up, looking happy.

"So, you have your tickets, and may I say, after you." My mother and I started walking up to gangplank with excitement in our steps. Then I looked back. I noticed that Collin was staring off into the distance. I didn't know why, but for some reason, I still cared. So, I doubled back and waved my hands in his face. I had a slight amount of difficulty doing this because I was short and he was tall. In return, he grabbed a handful of my fiery red hair and tossed it around.

"Hey!" I yelled. "What did you do that for?"

"Oh, sorry!" he yelled back in the most sarcastic voice ever. After that, no one said anything. We all were marveling at the ship. Everything was so delicately placed, so pretty, dramatic. The gold staircase was my favorite. As my family and I walked up to the first class area, I saw my mum and dad taking off in a different direction.

"Mum, Dad, aren't our rooms this way?" I said pointing to the hallway behind me.

"Oh yes," my dad replied, "We decided that you and your brother could stay together and spend some time getting to know each other better during the trip."

"What!" I nearly screamed. "I already know him perfectly fine." When you have a really nice house and your parents basically desert you every day, you have no choice but to get to know the people around you. I think that after one year or so of this, I know my brother well enough. But I just went with it. I had to. And so, I was on the Titanic stuck with my brother.

We found our room and decided to get dressed for dinner. I pulled a dress out of my trunk and put it on. Collin actually helped me tie a bow into my hair.

As we ate dinner, I felt lonely. My brother was talking to kids his age at the table and well, let's just say that you don't find many 11-year-old girls in a dining room full of boys. Finally, I slipped away to the library. It was beautiful! There were so many books. And about everything, too. Astronomy, science, math, everything. I spent hours in there. Until I heard footsteps.

Great, probably my brother coming to get me to go to bed, I thought. But, I was wrong. In entered a young lady. She had dressed appropriately, and she looked as if she was looking for something.

"Oh, hi," she said. She didn't looked surprised to see me. "What are you doing in the library this late at night?"

"Yeah, I had to get away. You see my brother, Collin..." And I was off. I was spilling all of my deepest secrets to a total stranger, but she didn't seem to mind. She just listened, and it felt nice. After I finished, she started talking.

"You might be wondering why I am here."

"Yeah, kind of."

"Well, you see I am a crystal gazer." This, as you might imagine, came as a shock, but it made sense, as she knew that I would be here.

"What?!" I half asked, half-yelled.

"Yes, and I saw that on April 14, 1921, at 11:40 PM the Titanic will hit an iceberg and will sink in 2 hours and 40 minutes on April 15, 1921. I also saw you here. According to my ball, you are the smartest of your age. I thought that you could help to avoid the disaster."

"Sure. But, why me? There are plenty of scientists on board. I'm just a kid."

"I know, that's why I choose you. I am in room 219." She walked out of the library. I was still utterly in shock, and that had given me no answer. But still, I couldn't ignore this.

***

That night, I was restless. I couldn't sleep. I kept thinking about what she had told me. I was thinking of all of the bad things that could happen and how many people that could die if I failed. Seriously, my family could die. I mean, the Titanic was 883 feet long, and there were 2,208 people on the Titanic. If something was going to happen, the Titanic would sink in just a short bit of time, and tons of people would die.

***

The next day came in a blur. It probably was because we were doing the same thing, or because of the information that I was told last night. I tried telling my brother all day, but he was too busy and wasn't interested in talking. Since, I hadn't seen my parents, I saw no point in even thinking about talking to them.

Before I knew it, the night of April 14, 1921, was approaching. As you might imagine, I couldn't sleep, again. I tossed and turned, and finally, I resorted to journaling. As I got out of bed, I only managed to stub my toe twice and hit my head, once. I grabbed a pen and a ballpoint pen, and I wrote.

Dear Diary,

As the hours are ticking down until 11:40 pm, all I can think of are all the terrible things that could happen. What if the woman was just telling me a lie and nothing is actually going to happen? Or, what if when I am trying to do something, I fall off the ship, get pneumonia, and die? Or, I fall asleep (though I highly doubt that that could happen) and sleep through it all, and then I drown and wake up in heaven? I can only think about these things. I can't sleep, and I can't anything. Well, I might as well wake up my brother, tell him what is happening, and hope that he doesn't laugh at me and kick me out of the room. Until next time.

Regards,
Alizah

When I was done with this, I realized that it was 11:00 pm.

Okay, I have exactly 40 minutes to tell my brother and save the Titanic. I walked over to my brother's bed. This time only stubbing my toe once. I shook him awake.

"What's happening, where am I?"

"Collin, listen in 40 minutes, the Titanic is going to hit an iceberg, and the Titanic will sink in about 2 hours and 40 minutes."

"Alizah, where could you have gotten a silly idea like that? Besides, I just wanna sleep. Goodnight." I tried to wake him again, but it was clear that he didn't care.

Fine, he doesn't want to help me. Well, I guess I will do it myself. I walked to room 219. I knocked quietly on the door. A few seconds later, it was opened by the woman from the library.

"Good, you came!" she said in an excited voice.

"Yeah."

"Come, we mustn't waste time. We have less than 20 minutes to get the captain and tell him that we must go another way." She grabbed onto my arm, and we ran. We ran like the wind. All the way to the captain's quarters. By the time that we got there, I was out of breath, but I didn't care. I knocked firmly on the door. It was opened by a tired captain.

"What's happening? Is it a 10-31?" The captain asked.

"No captain, it isn't a 10-31 or whatever that is." By this point, the captain was staring at us in pure amazement. He ushered us in and asked up what we were doing there.

"Well, you see, I am Elizabeth and this is?"

"Alizah," I said.

"Alright, but I still don't know why you are here." And both were off. We were taking turns explaining everything. By the time that we did, the captain stood thunderstruck, just as I had been. But he believed us. I didn't think he would, but still, he did. At that moment, the telegraph boy came running in.

"Captain," he said out of breath. "I have just received a telegram from another ship. They are surrounded by ice. And if we keep going in this direction, we will crash into an iceberg."

"Thank you. We have already received this news." He nodded towards us. We will change direction immediately." The boy ran out, and the captain turned to us.

"Thank you. You have saved many lives tonight." He ushered us out and gave a short nod.

We walked back to our rooms, firsts hers. Then, I walked to mine. I was thinking about why he had believed us. I guess it was because he didn't want to be bothered, and he figured that agree with us would be the best way not to be bothered. Or because he thought that we were trustworthy and that we should be trusted. Whatever. I thought. Then I walked into my brother standing there.

"Did it go well?"

"What?" I asked with pure curiosity.

"Saving the Titanic, of course."

"I thought you didn't even care."

"Of course! I'm your brother, and you're my sister. I have to care. I love you." This time, there was no sarcastic voice. I could tell that he meant what he said. He held out his hands as to give me a hug, and I wrapped mine around him.

"I love you, too." We parted and smiled. I started walking back to my bed, and he walked to his. I dreamed about the most amazing brother ever. A brother named Collin.

The next morning I woke up, and Collin and I went to breakfast. It was different that day, I got to pick what to do, and Collin didn't say anything. It seemed as if he was having fun. I figured he was. Every day left was like that.

Finally, the last night on the ship, Collin and I were talking about our plans in the United States. As we got in our beds, Collin asked, "You know, what you did today, was the sign of a mature young lady. You're so, so brave. Don't you feel a little bit like bragging?"

"I don't know," I said, "I guess it wasn't a small thing that I did, but I realize that there are more important things in life to focus on. Not just the things that make you feel great, but the things that make you great."

Collin was quiet for a moment. Then he said, "You know, I have never been more proud of you. And,

I don't know what I would do without you." Then the light went out, and I fell asleep to my thoughts.

He really does care about me. I don't know what I would do without him. Or my parents for that matter. I'm glad we all survived together.

ABOUT THE AUTHOR *Hi, I am Mary Grace. I am 11 years old in 6th grade at Summit Middle School. In my spare time, I love writing, playing the piano, drawing, baking, cooking, and READING! I hope that y'all enjoyed reading my story!*

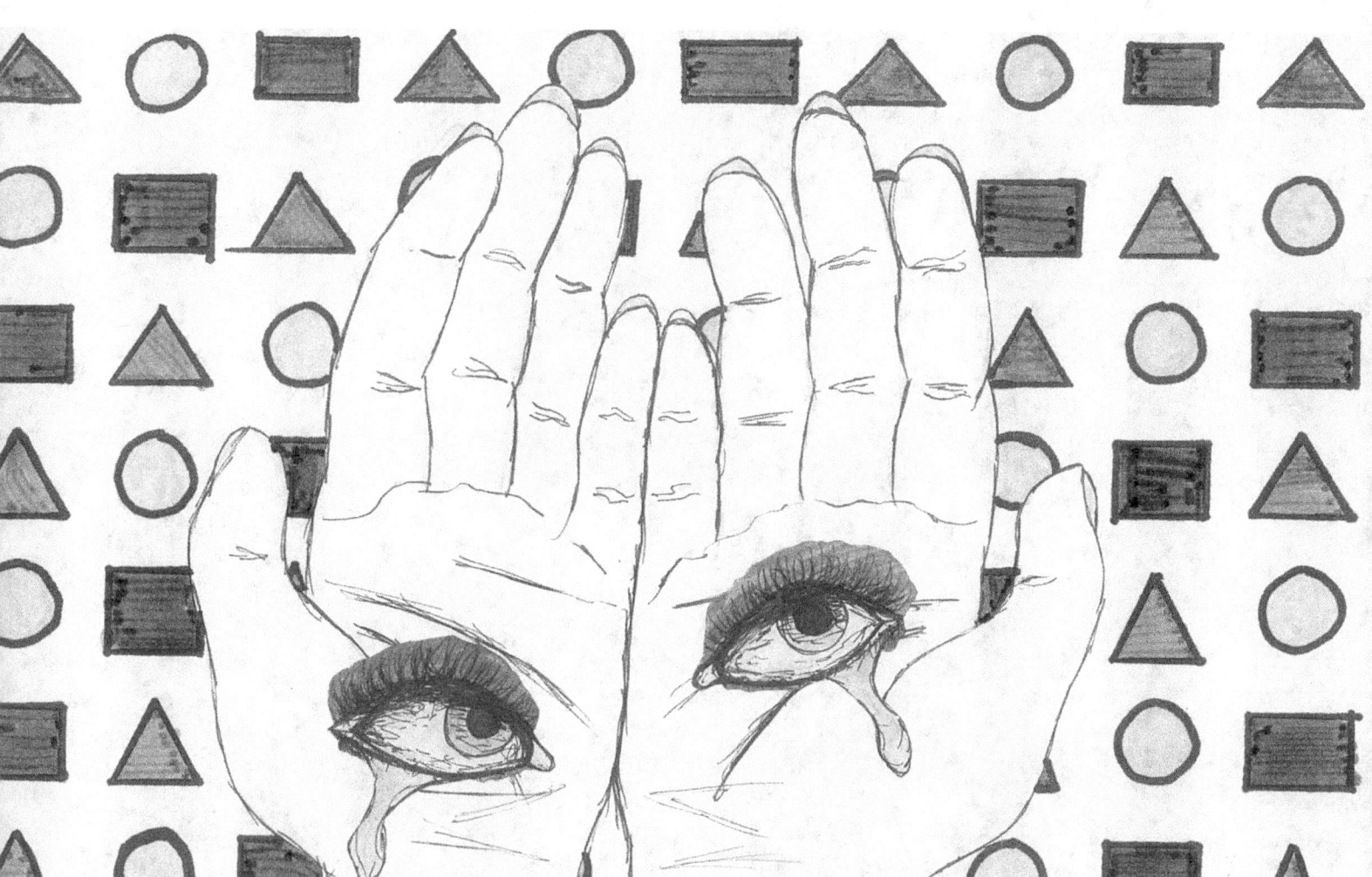

Expressive Eyes
Mixed Media | Amber Walsh, Grade 11

I grew up around my father who was constantly drawing and painting when I was little. He would paint murals for our church and paint at home. It was just always in my life, and I loved it. Now that I'm older, art still has a heavy influence over my life between my dad and my girlfriend, who also is an artist that I'm always looking up to because her work is absolutely amazing. Whether or not my piece is particularly good or not, I am proud of it very simply because I'm happy to be a part of something that both of these very important people have shared with me, and now I get to share that with more people as well.

Aspen Forest Zentangles

Mixed Media | Mackenna Simson, Grade 10

As I created this piece of art, what came to mind was my backyard: an aspen forest. This forest was where my twin sister Logan and I spent a lot of our summer days as little kids, indulging in new adventures and enjoying the abundance of life, where we played many, many games. Through this piece, I wanted to capture not only the physical depth of the forest, but also the intellectual depth, which help the people looking at my drawing to think about the memories associated with the forest. There is so much more than just trees in this forest. The zentangle helped me to communicate those ideas. It helped me to express how much more is associated with this specific bunch of aspen trees because within the detail, there is more detail. This piece was created at Summit High School and was based off of the zentangle landscape assignment. I have always loved to draw and paint, although this is the only drawing class I have taken. I am a sophomore, and have lived in Summit County for my entire life, and thus am heavily influenced by the beauty of nature. Other influences in my life include my parents, sister, and friends. I have enjoyed the class that I am taking, and hope that my future will be focused on or guided by art.

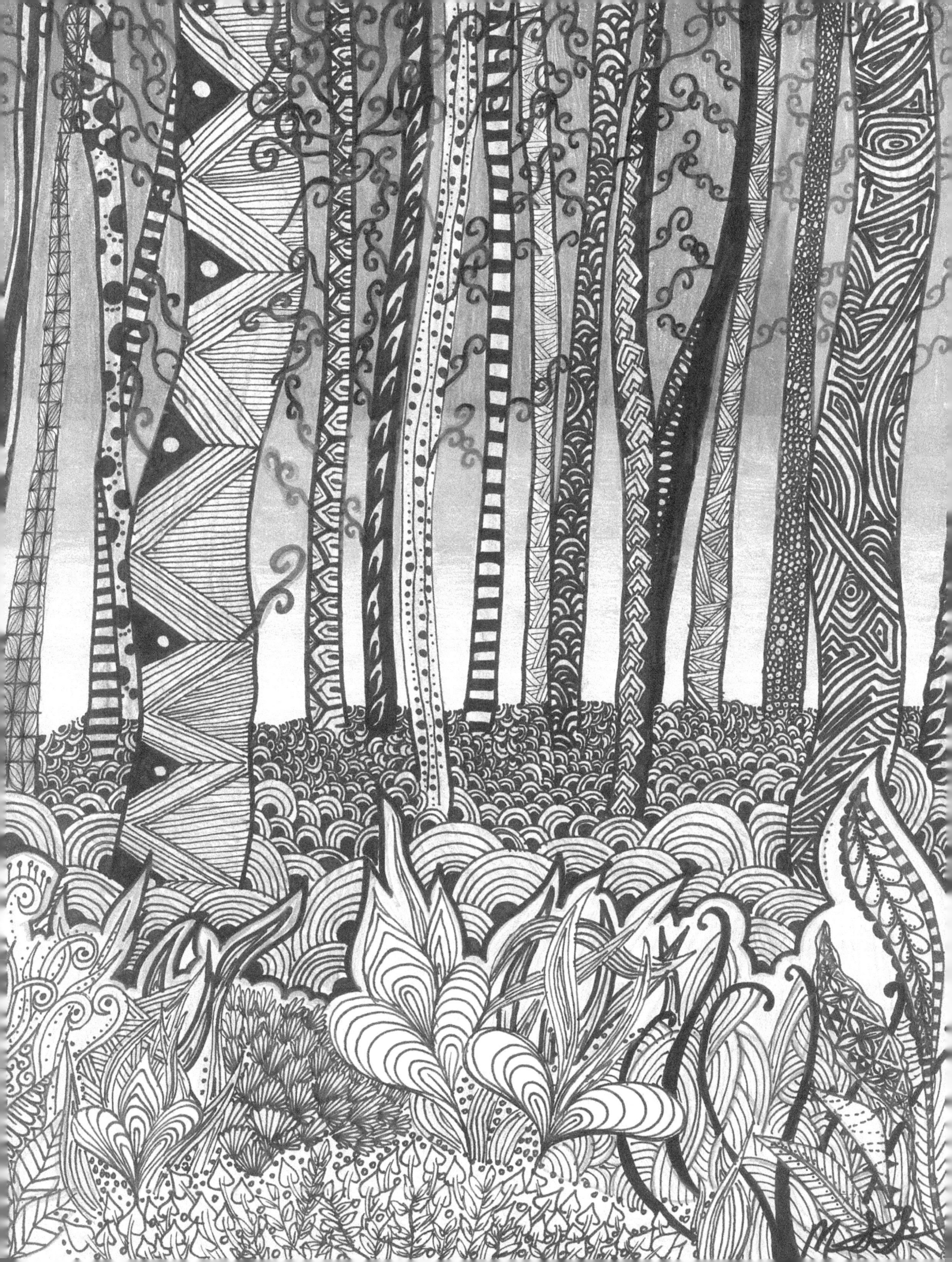

Oh, What Would I Do Without You?

By Anya Waldes

You were given this life because you are strong enough to live it.

I was just an ordinary second grader. Obsessed with the new thing and playing kickball at recess. I loved my family and hanging out with friends. I was just a normal 6 year old girl with an ordinary 2nd grader life…or so I thought.

At the time, I had a 5 year old sister. I loved her more than anything… sometimes. As sisters, you know, we had our problems, but we were sisters, and that will never change.

Neither will the fact that my life was drastically altered one night about that time 4 years ago. It was just a regular school night, and I was getting on my pajamas and kissing my dad and sister goodnight. I got into bed and surrounded myself with covers and all of the stuffed animals that I could find. Before my head hit the pillow, I was fast asleep and dreamin'.

It was pitch black, and someone slipped their hands under my back and lifted me off of my bed, my fuzzy pink blanket wrapping me up. I didn't know what was going on, but I was still groggy and half-asleep. The unknown human being that had a grip on me carried me outside.

Suddenly, I was blinded by flashing lights and people rushing around, but a second later, everything disappeared, and I blacked out. The next morning, I woke up in a stranger's house, with the light streaming through the window.

I walked downstairs, and I realized that I was in my neighbor's house. I asked what was going on, and they told me that something had happened, and that my sister was sick. I walked back over to my house, and my dad had left a note. It said, "We had to take your sister to the doctor, but everything is fine."

Even then, I knew that everything was not fine, and it might not be for a while. I went to school that day anxious and confused. It was the first time that I had been away from my baby sister and had not been able to protect her from the world.

It was shocking to learn that my sister had had a seizure, and at that time, I really didn't even know what it was. I soon learned that the seizure was over 16 hours long, and if my dad had caught it any later, I could've lost the one person that I love the most in my life. It had already caused a lot of damage to her health, and she was in a coma for many days. I wasn't allowed to see her for a while because it was a really intense scene of her in the hospital, so my parents thought it was best if I waited a little while until everything was under control. When I did see her, I was taken aback. I guess, I didn't really imagine that she could be really that sick, but I was proved wrong. It was a little altering to see her lying there in a coma with all of the wires and medical equipment around her. I had to stay positive when I was in my sister's room. I would talk to her, sing to her, play music for her, really just letting her know that I was there for her. It was even to help me deal with what was going on and help me deal with my emotions.

It was another whole life living without my partner in crime. My life was a little bit of a frenzy without my rock right by my side.

Even through all of this, I learned who I was because of one little girl. I had always wanted to be a doctor. It started off with the doctor kits and giving my family shots to make them feel better. I always wanted to help people.

When I saw my sister in the hospital with so many other children around her, I knew that there were so many other children that were in the same situation as her. She inspired me to become someone that people could count on to give them a second chance at life.

I realized that nobody is here forever, and things can disappear so much sooner than you would ever imagine. I mean, I had always loved my family, but I had never realized how important it is to show that love until I almost lost my best friend. I know that my sister may not be the ordinary 9-year old sister, but she sure is an amazing human being and has helped me discover who I am and who I want to become.

ABOUT THE AUTHOR *Hey, my name is Anya Waldes, and I am a 6th grade girl working out my future career at Summit Middle School. I have a beautiful 9-year sister who has helped me through so much. I have amazing and supportive parents and friends. I like to be really athletic, and I love playing Volleyball and competing in Gymnastics. I enjoy some downtime as well. I love sitting down and reading or journaling about my life experiences. I absolutely adore traveling, and I try to take as many opportunities to do just that as I can.*

Imagine Feeling Loved

Pen and Ink
Natalie Leyva, Grade 11

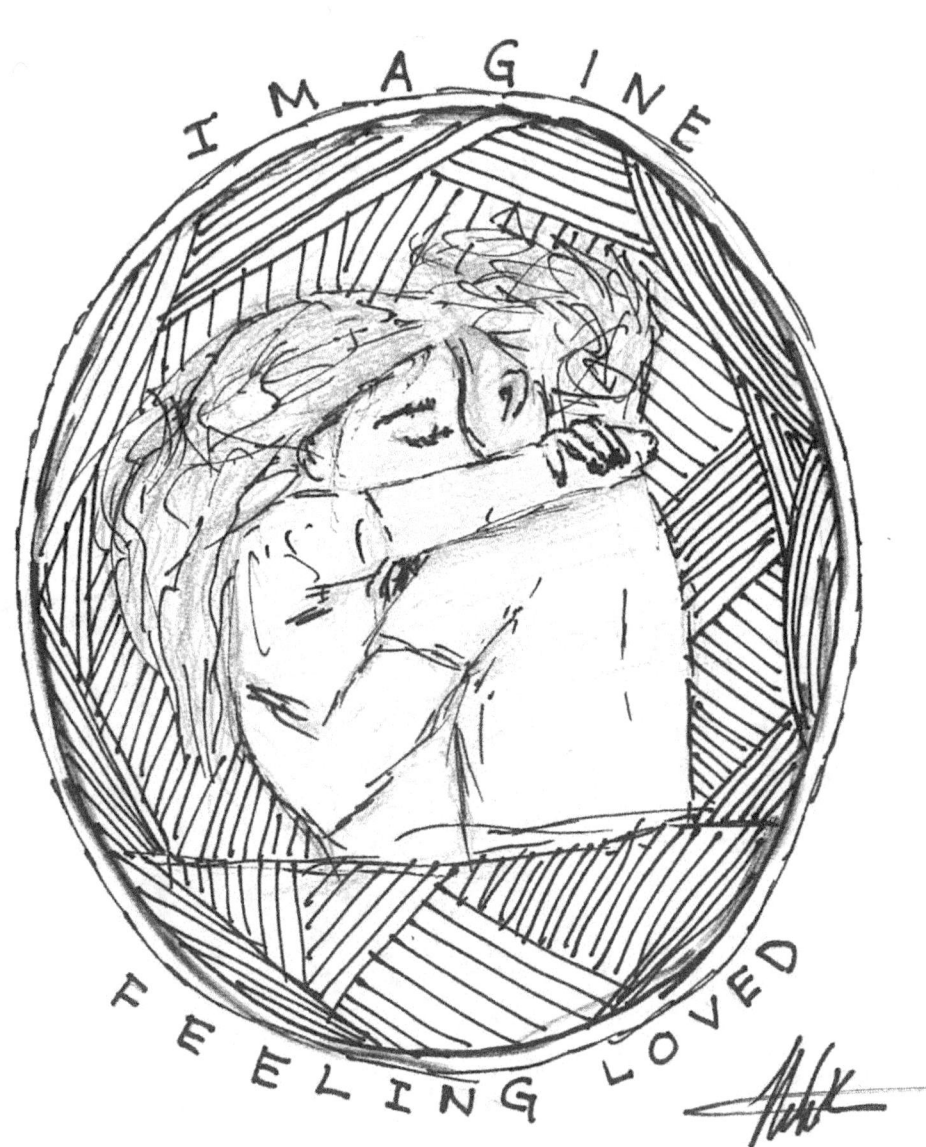

Teton Barn

**Mixed Media
Oliver Trowbridge,
Grade 11**

My name is Oliver Trowbridge. I am currently in 11th grade at Summit High School, and I was born and raised in Breckenridge. I have grown up loving the outdoors, hunting, and fishing. I enjoy drawing because I can let all of the ideas out of my brain and onto the paper. I like to use pencil to draw, and when it's done, I stand back and gaze at my masterpiece.

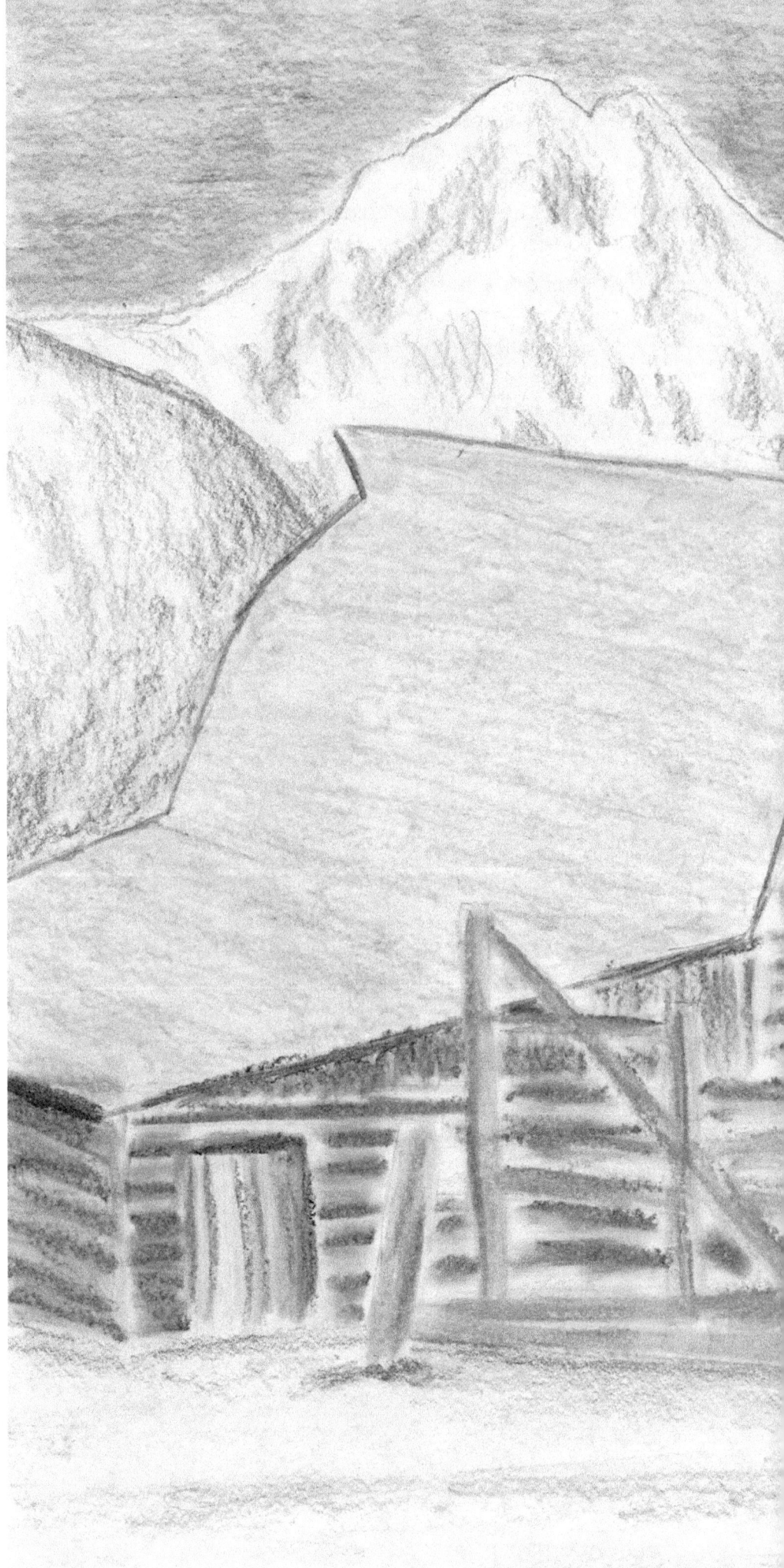

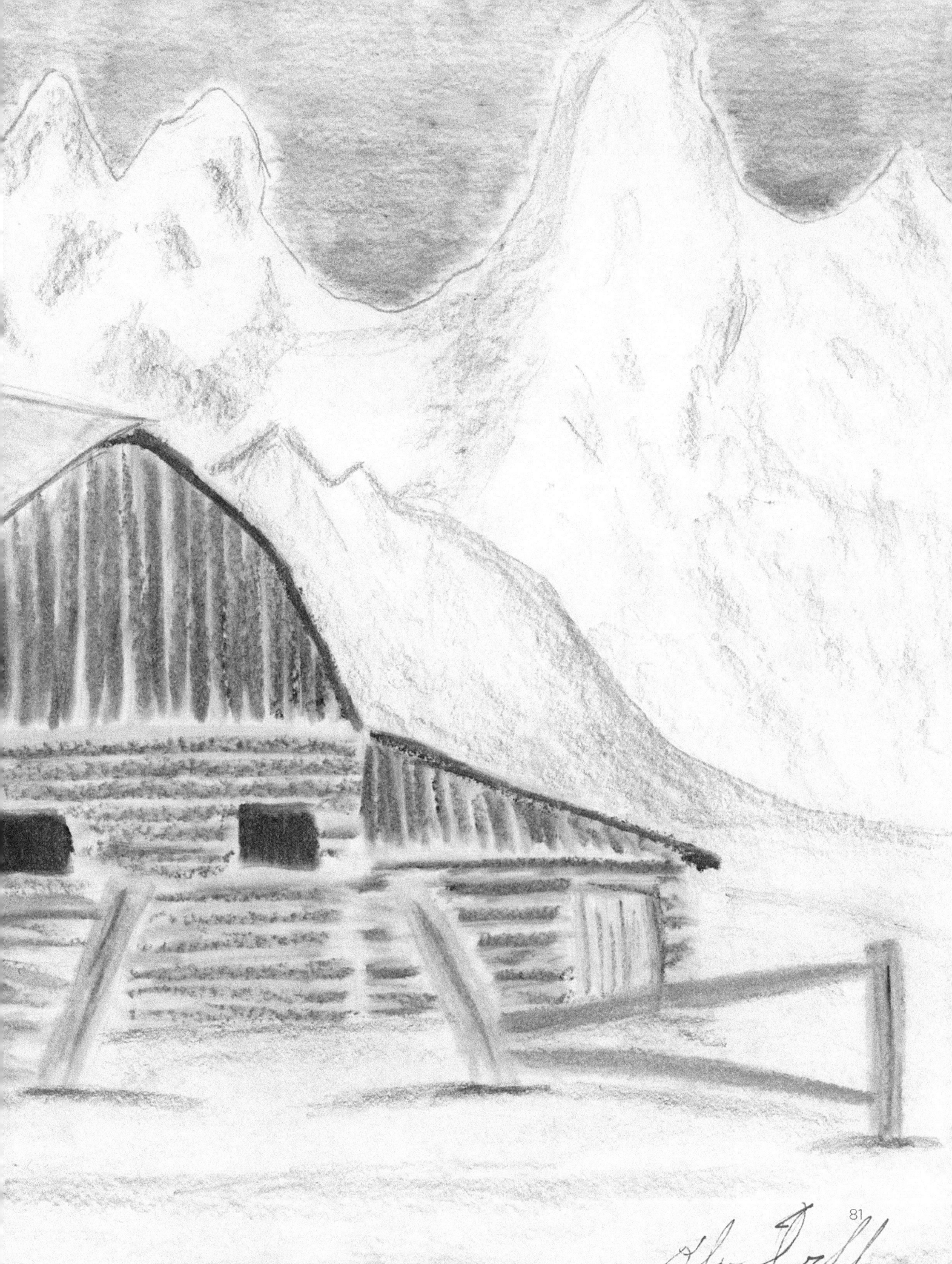

Bowie

Pen | Gwen Goodenbour, Grade 10

Hi, my name Gwen, and I am currently a high school sophomore. I am an intern for BreckCreate and will be soon transitioning into a studio assistant position. I love creating art and am always aspiring to further educate myself.

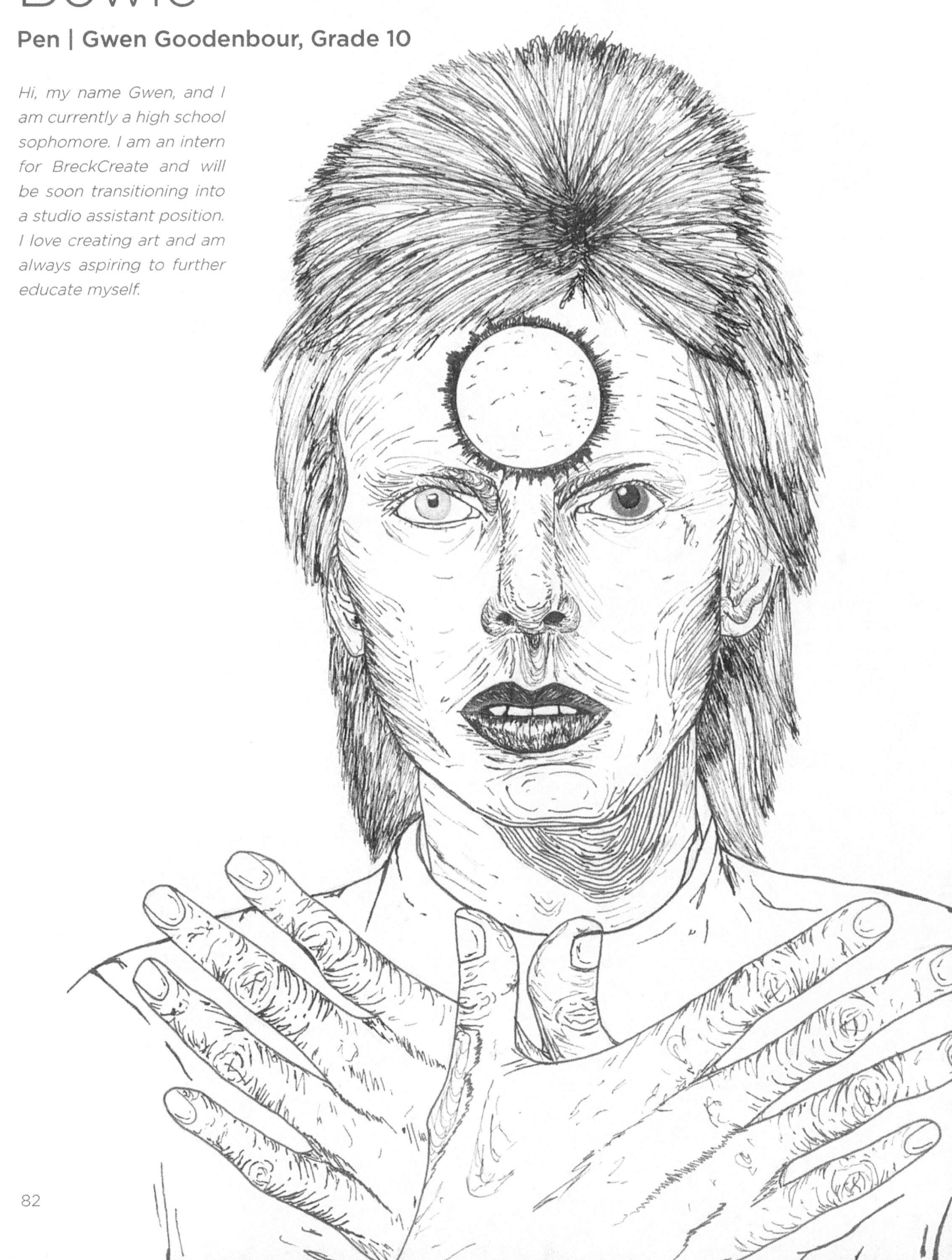

The Dreams
By Mandy Clawson

Oh, where to start! It was all the same, you see. Wake up, go to school, eat, come home from work, eat, sleep, repeat. I tried to change it, to mix things up, but nothing ever worked well. I didn't have any friends. I was the senior that sat by himself during lunch. But not anymore. It all started with them. The life-changers. Mark, Josh, and Ron.

I was forced to attend a party at a karaoke bar with my choir class in college. I didn't take the class because I was good at singing, but just for the extra credit. And since Mr. Sinclaire counted it as a grade, I would've failed the class if I hadn't gone. He made everyone either sing solo or duet at least once. Because I had no friends, I obviously sang solo. For the simple reason that I legitimately didn't care, I put the song choice to shuffle and was stuck with Carrie Underwood's "Jesus Take the Wheel." I croaked out the lyrics as I read them on screen, then sat in the back with a beer I snatched from the counter. It was then that he approached me. His name was Mark. He stood tall, confident, with sandy brown hair and bright green eyes, a smile so bright it could blind you.

I had raised an eyebrow at him and let him sit when he asked to.

"Dude, your singing is awesome." he said. I nodded and grunted out a "thank you." He sat up straighter and put his hands down on the table in front of him.

"I know we don't know each other, but it'd be sick if we made a band. We'd be called, 'Unreal.'"

Now, I might add that I was at a point in my life where I really didn't care what happened next, and I sort of just went along with things, so I agreed, and he insisted on taking me to show me some stuff right then and there. So, I followed him. Because what's the worst a twenty-something guy's gonna do? A whole lot worse than I thought, but we'll get there eventually.

So we get to his place, and I listen to his stuff. The music, the drums, guitar, bass, was amazing. But the singer sounded like a strangled rat. As I was completely apathetic towards my future, I said, "screw it," took over as the lead singer, and started practicing right then and there with his band.

I learned the lyrics, hummed them in the hallways, belted them in my room, and sang them in my head, all day, every day. Weeks passed, and we recorded several songs, but I had no one to play them for, and other people largely ignored us, so we never got noticed.

I suggested that we pick up some gigs around town, but it never really worked out. After a while, I dropped it, but I still really enjoyed making music. When I finally graduated from college, I was 21. We became roommates and continued doing what we loved. We would blast our music throughout the small apartment and go out almost every night. Although, I think it was just for him to laugh and watch me get drunk, as he didn't drink at all.

It was just me and him he until we met Josh. Josh had a sort of baby look about him. He looked so innocent and wore bright pastel colors. He was truly the nicest person you could meet. We met him at a bar, and he was talking to a huge crowd. I noticed him because I never could've talked to that many people at once. Mark befriended him, and I warmed up to him quickly. Mark told him about the band, and Josh agreed to play drums.

So then there were three. A couple months later, we were at a concert with one of our favorite bands. We'd bought backstage tickets, but only because Mark wanted them. So, the concert ended, and we were backstage talking to people, and then we met Ron. He was sitting in a back booth with his feet up on the table to reveal huge 6-inch heels. Ron had a look that just kind of screamed, "I'll sass you, don't test me." He had neat stubble and wore approximately 3 lbs of makeup around his brown eyes alone. To be fair, it was flawless, but if you told him, he'd just nod and say, "I know." He had tight clothes, too, that couldn't have been comfortable. His confidence radiated.

He joined our band as the bass guitar. We were amazing. Ron added that finishing touch, completing the band's personality. He also had a thick Louisiana accent, which made him fun to listen to. He tried talking with a northern accent, which always got a laugh. He did most of the talking in the group for a while, but he eventually made me talk to people and become more confident. In a way, they were all teaching me how to better myself. Mark taught me how to look good, Ron taught me how to feel good, and Josh taught me how to make others feel good. They really helped me.

Years flew by, and I was twenty-six now, a long way from the shy senior I was in high school. I had a great group of friends in Mark, Ron, and Josh. I'd been working at a grocery store, but they let me go since I spent so much time with the band. We never did anything but sing and play. But in one night, it all fell apart.

Three of us were sleeping, and Josh came in the door, yelling and covered in blood. We helped him calm down as he said over and over, "It isn't my blood. It's not my fault." I wasn't sure which was worse. The fact that it wasn't his blood, or that he felt the need to tell us it wasn't his fault. What did he do? He passed out, dead asleep, and we got him into bed, but Mark wouldn't let me call the police until we spoke to him. But the next morning, all three acted as if it had never happened.

"It was probably just a dream," said Mark.

"You really think I'd kill someone?" asked Josh.

"I think you're just crazy," added Ron.

And I believed them. I reassured myself it was just a dream, until it happened two more times with Mark and Ron. I thought to myself, *just a dream, just a recurring nightmare. Nothing to worry about. It's fine.*

One day as we were walking home, Mark told us he thought we should move away, as there'd been an incredibly high rate of deaths around this town recently. People stabbed, mauled, strangled, and cut up. It was ridiculously gruesome, and I agreed. We should move. Before long, we were in the city.

The nightmares haunted me for months, even after we moved away. But then, in one of the dreams, it was me who came home covered in blood. And I remembered what I did in my dream for days. I found a younger red-headed girl, about seventeen, and I stabbed her, repeatedly, I couldn't stop. I remember the feeling, because there wasn't one. No grief, no guilt, not even satisfaction. Just nothing. And in my dream, when I returned home, they met me at the door and asked me how it felt. They seemed excited. I was numb.

The dreams went on for so long, I learned to ignore them and just not worry about it anymore. That is, until I found an old newspaper article about the red-headed girl in my dream. At least, that's what Ron said. He told me the girl fit the description of the girl I described. I thought it was a funny coincidence until I actually read it.

> *Martha Waters, 16, was found dead, her face torn to shreds, yesterday morning near Hart Park.*

I honestly freaked out. The pictures were before and after her death, *and it was legitimately the girl I'd dreamed about.* But it was just a dream, it had to have been. I didn't kill anybody.

I ran. I opened the door and ran. Mark, Josh, and Ron chased me for so long, and they finally caught up to me at the entrance to Hart Park. I ran up to the first police officer I saw and showed them the article, demanding information. My three friends all tried to talk at once, and I finally snapped.

I turned, screaming at them.

"I dreamt about killing this girl, and you're trying to tell me 'It's probably nothing'? No! I won't take it anymore." I turned to the large female cop, and was taken aback when she stared at me as if I was insane. I sighed.

"Look ma'am, I know that sounded bad, but my friends here," I gestured behind me, "won't shut up, and I've been stressing for so long. I-" the cop held up a finger as she cut me off.

"Sir, I need you to calm down. Start over. Who are you talking to? We're the only ones here." I stared at her. Turning back to my friends, they had the same confused look on their faces.

"No, no, you must understand." I pointed to each of them. "This is Mark..." I realized I didn't know his last name, or any of theirs for that matter. I moved on, denying it.

"And there's Josh, and Ron's there with the makeup." The cop sighed and called for backup in her walkie talkie. I was really starting to panic now. I turned to Mark, but they'd disappeared. I turned back to the cop, and she held up a hand.

"Sir, I'm going to have to ask you to lie down and put your hands behind your back."

***

"And now you're here," says Dr. Jenner. I nod.

"And it's safe to assume I'm talking to Derek right now?" he asks. I raise an eyebrow.

"Duh, that's my name, isn't it?" I ask, trying to make a joke. He shrugs.

"Well yesterday I talked to Josh, and he told me a different story. The day before that I talked to Ron, and a different one from him," he says, matter of fact. "I have yet to talk to Mark."

I scoff and focus on his small porcelain man on his desk. "Well, you'd obviously be able to tell who I am, we all look different. Or, sorry, are you...?" I analyze his dark glasses. "Are you blind?" I ask him. He shakes his head, scribbling on his notesheet.

"And, Derek," says Dr. Jenner, "you are the original? You remember life before you met in the karaoke bar?" I nod.

"Obviously, but it was super boring. I hated school." Dr. Jenner nods again, writing in his notes more.

"Did you ever *touch* any of your friends?"

"Seriously? That's a ridiculous question."

He tilts his head and continued.

"Can I hear some of your music?" I thought back while I pulled out my iPod for the music we recorded. Surely we touched at some point, I knew them for years. I plug earbuds into the iPod and hand it to Dr. Jenner, and I help him set it on one of our songs. He listens and writes more, then looks up at me.

"Have you ever listened to this? It's just you singing. No other instruments." I shake my head. I start to say no, but I can hear the music through the earbuds because it's so loud on his lap.

It's only me singing. He's right. Dr. Jenner sighs.

"Derek Critch, you have been accused of over 50 counts of third degree murder, and now, I must officially diagnose you with Dissociative Identity Disorder. In my recommendation to the court, you are not fit to stand trial. "

No.

"Good luck, Mr. Critch."

ABOUT THE AUTHOR *My name is Mandy Clawson. I'm in 9th grade at Summit High School, and I'm in advanced classes for Math and Science. I moved here about 3 years ago from Arkansas. I enjoy reading, writing, and creating art. I really like horror movies and psychological fiction.*

Wheelin' Around the World

**Identity Photogram
Johnny Lunney,
Grade 10**

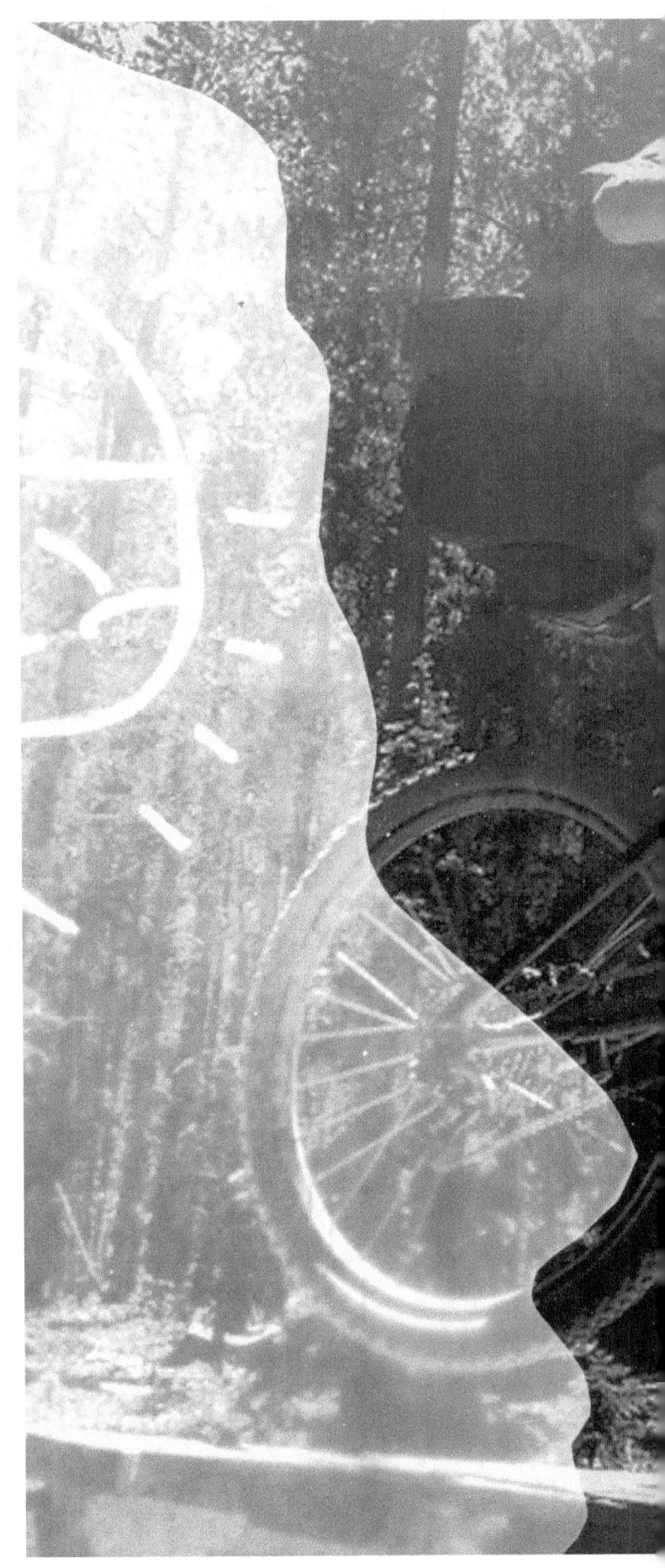

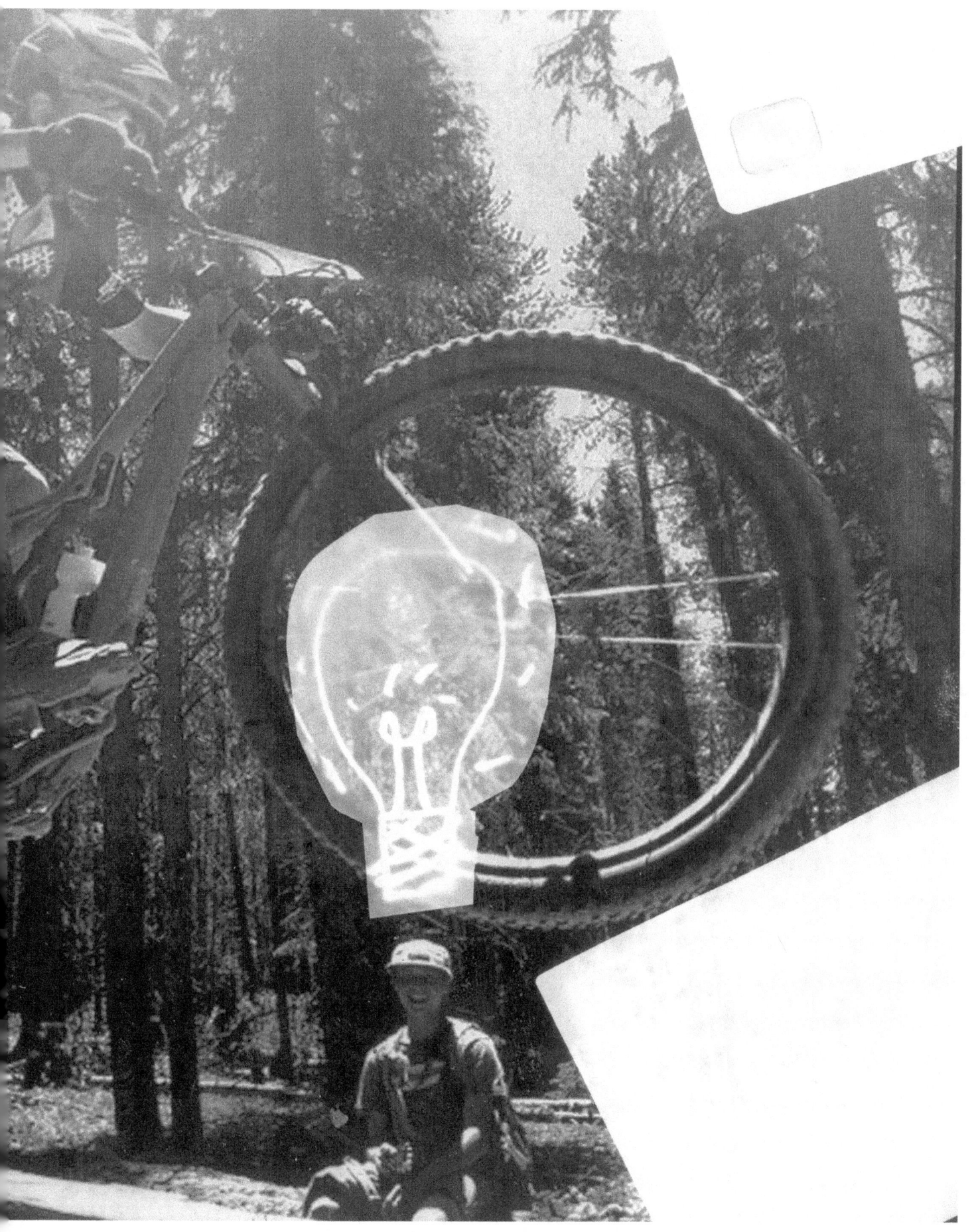

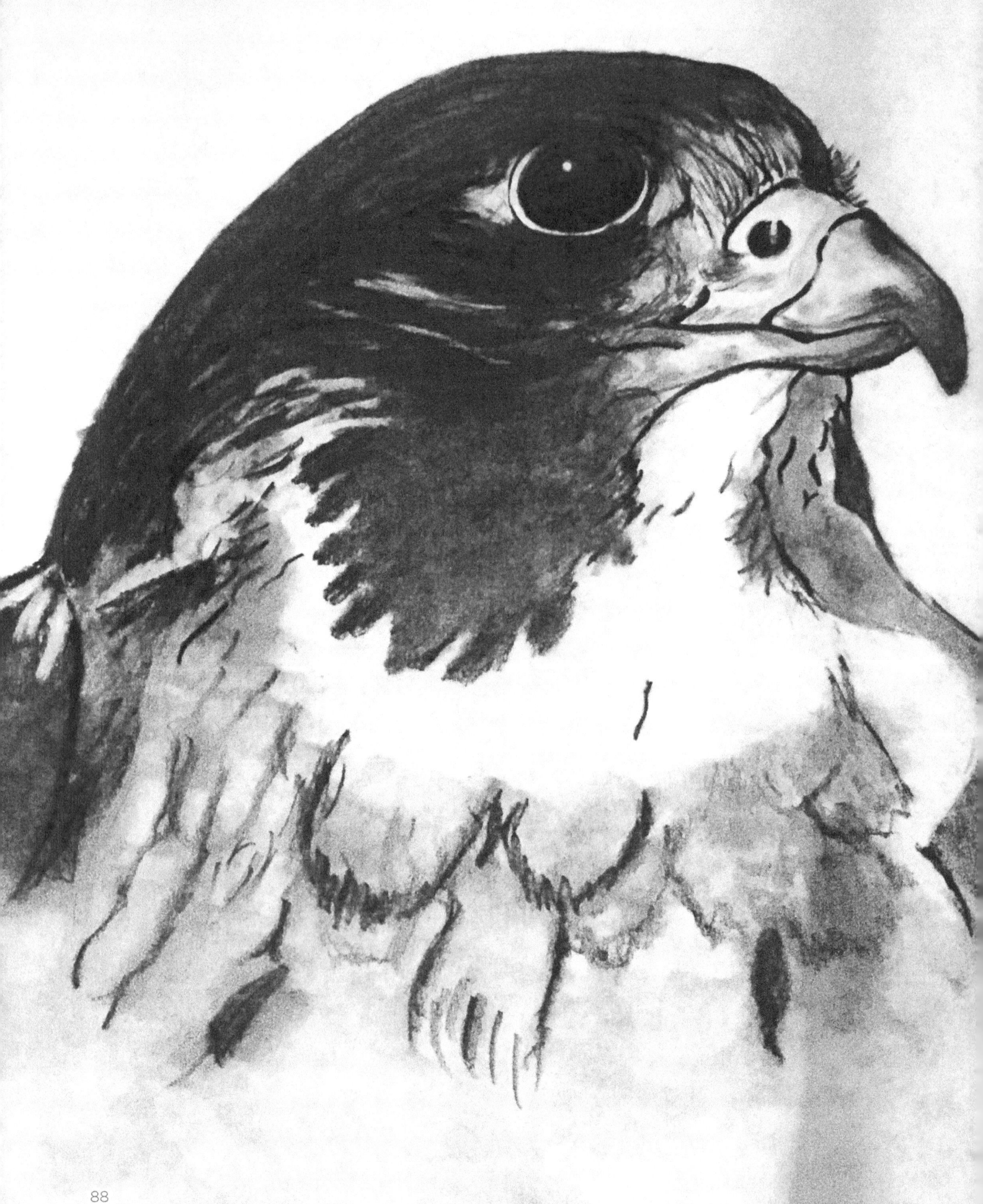

Peregrine Falcon

Graphite | Isaac Dalrymple, Grade 8

My name is Isaac Dalrymple, and I am in 8th grade at Summit Middle School, CO. I've been drawing for as long as I can remember and drew this when I was in 6th grade. It is my favorite piece because I have always had a deep love for birds as well. I also love to yoyo, play guitar, lacrosse, and most of all snowboard. Last year I was the artist of the month as well as the first ever P.E. MVP.

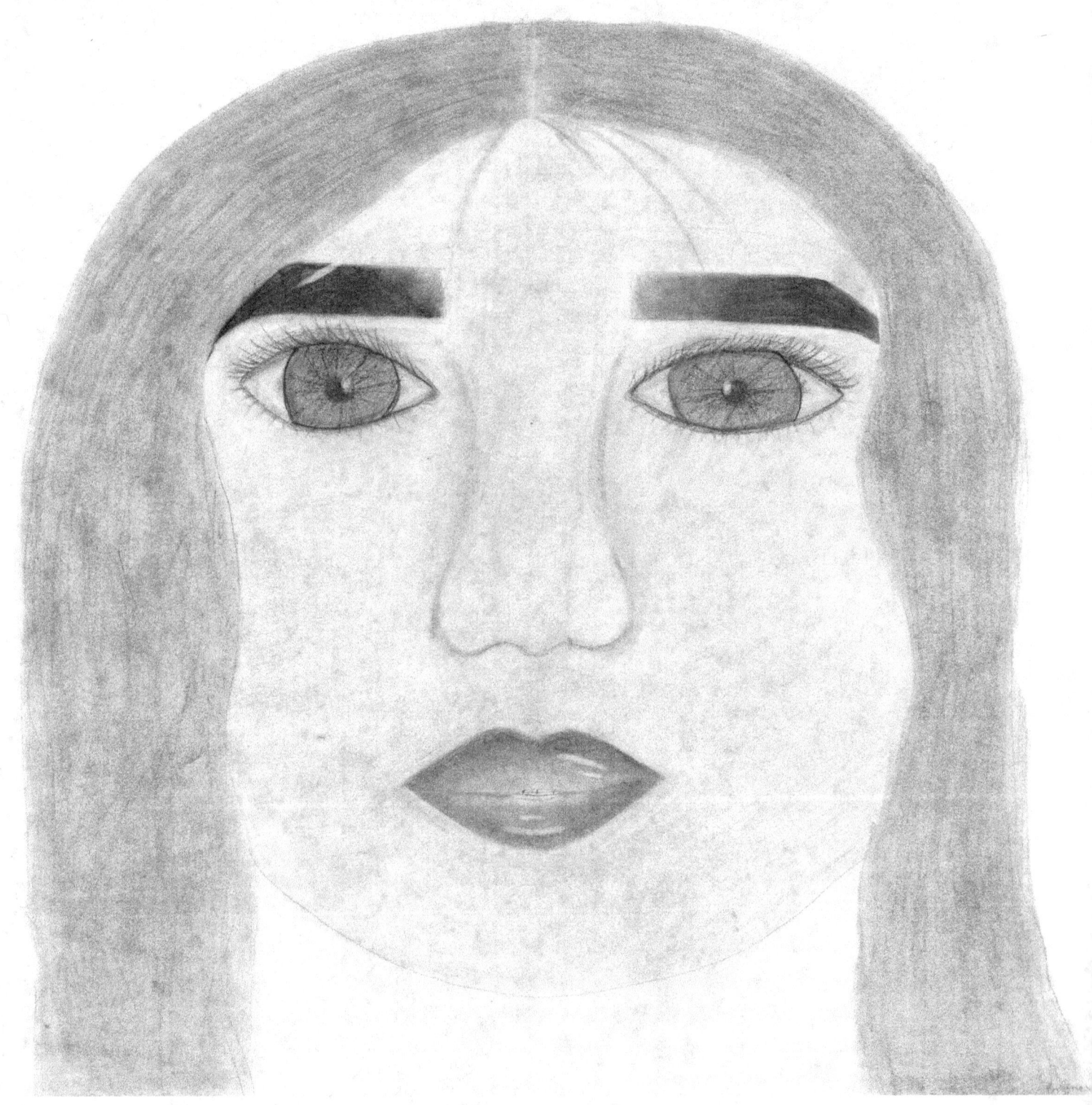

Self-Portrait

Graphite | Britney Venegas, Grade 9

I am 15 years old. I grew up in Silverthorne, CO but was born in Denver on January 14th. In middle school I took two art classes. For my drawing, I used a mixed medium. I chose to use a colored pencil for the eyes to make them the main focus. I love making art because it helps me draw what's on my mind and relieve stress. My artwork is about how I feel and my point of view of a special topic.

Spy
By Ella Meltzer

One day, there was a young school boy sitting on a bench in a normal park, eating a normal lunch on a normal day.

But that was all about to change.

That seemingly normal boy's name was Nicholas Martin. And he was anything but normal. Nicholas was a twelve year old spy for the Russian government. He had been recruited after his father Michael Martin, who was also a Russian spy, was killed by Russian terrorists.

The spy organization Nicholas works for is the Widows. They are snipers, assassins, and undercover killers. Nicholas happened to be recruited as an undercover killer. The Widows basically kill off powerful people who might be a threat. The enemy is anyone and everyone powerful because powerful people could potentially do bad things to the Russians.

Nicholas is in London, England. His mission: To kill the prime minister of England, Grace Evans. She has no shortage of power and influence, and just a month ago she broke the UK's trade relations with Russia. In the 21st century Russia has been struggling in their economy, so they could not let Evans take away their trade relations with England. So their president Malcolm Petrov had sent in Nicholas to get the job done, and that was exactly what he was going to do.

He first had to stay undercover for about a month before the assassination so nobody suspected anything.

The time had come. The kill was about to happen.

Ch. 2 - Recruit

Nicholas Martin and his father Michael were sitting in their small home in Murmansk, Russia playing their favorite game of chess at the dining room table. Nicholas was winning - he had two of his father's pawns and one of his rooks. Nicholas had a pale complexion, with brown eyes, and he was very tall. His father was the same, pale, brown eyes, and very, very tall. Michael had cared for Nicholas on his own since his mother had died during birth. Michael was a tough father, grooming his child to be just like him - hard, emotionless, and deadly.

Michael was off duty when it happened.

Suddenly, there was a giant explosion. Nicholas and Michael both knew at the same time. Terrorists had attacked Murmansk! They ran out the door, and on their way out, Michael grabbed the pistol that he kept under the hollow plant pot on their porch. Just in case.

Then a bullet came out of nowhere and hit Michael right between the eyes. And he died just like that. A life of a living, breathing person just snuffed out like nothing.

Before Nicholas had time to go to his father, men in black suits appeared on either side of him. They put a bag over his head and dragged him to the Widow's secret base.

Location: Unknown

When the bag was pulled off, Nicholas could not see. Then a light turned on, and there was a man in a Russian military uniform sitting across from him. He said his name was Damien Mikhailov.

He then said, "Your father is dead, and you Nicholas have been recruited by the Widows to kill the enemy. Your training starts in two weeks." Then he left without another word.

Ch. 3 - Training

Nicholas has stayed in that room in the dark for what felt like at least a week without food or water. Then on what he thought might be the eighth day, another man in a black suit came in, put a bag over his head and dragged him out of the room.

He had been put in a car, and they drove for about a half hour. Then the door of the car opened, and he was pulled out. The minute he got out of the car, the sound of seagulls reached his ears, and the smell of salt permeated the air. He knew immediately he was at the shore.

They then put him on a boat and drove out to sea. After about an hour in the boat, they came to an abrupt stop. Then the bag was finally taken off. They were on a large rocky island with birds all over it.

Nicholas and the black suited man walked onto the island and stopped at a normal looking hill of jagged rocks. Then suddenly, a blinding light flashed right in his eye, but it was gone before Nicholas could see what had made the flash. Then the rock started to shift, and an entryway appeared. The black-suited man shoved Nicholas forward. Then the entry disappeared and so did the man.

Nicholas realized that the blinding light outside must have been a retinal scan. He stayed where he was - he had a feeling that someone would come for him. After about five minutes of waiting, the man from the dark room appeared.

He said, "Come Nicholas, we must talk." He took Nicholas to what might have been his office except instead of pictures of his family, he had guns hanging on the wall.

Damien Mikhailov. Apparently very relaxed, he sat down and put his feet up on his desk. Nicholas was on edge. Ready to spring up and run from the room. Mikhailov broke the silence.

"Before you ask. Nicholas, there is nothing you can do to get out of this. We both know that if you try, you will be killed." So, let's cut to the chase. "Your training starts tomorrow. You are going to take what we like to call a killer aptitude test. It will determine which category to put you in - either undercover killer, assassin, or sniper. One of my men will escort you to your cell, oh sorry, I meant room."

When the door of Mikhailov's Office was closed behind Nicholas, a man in black came out of the darkness and put a bag over his head again. He was then thrown unceremoniously into a room. The bag was pulled off, and he was once again alone. Nicholas thought that when Mikhailov had said it was a room, it really was more like a cell. There was a bed with no linens and a toilet without a lid.

The next morning Mikhailov appeared at Nicholas' cell door. He produced a key and unlocked the door. He came in and grabbed Nicholas by the elbow and dragged him out of the cell. This time there was no bag on his head. So it was the first good look he had had at the lair. There was not much to look at - the walls were white with no doors or corridors. But then a door appeared. Just one, and Mikhailov led Nicholas through it. There was one metal table and a counter with many large syringes.

"Are you ready for your killer aptitude test Nicholas?" Mikhailov asked.

"I think so."

Then a man in a white lab coat appeared, and Mikhailov left the room.

"Hello, my name is Dr. Arthro," said the man in the lab coat not unkindly. Arthro had a balding head with wispy white strands of hair. He was in his 60s, and he was very skinny. He looked as though a slight breeze could blow him away.

Then the Dr. beckoned to Nicholas to follow him. They went into a room that seemed to be an obstacle course.

"You have to go through this course. That is all. Then you will be done. You will get your results 30 minutes after the end of the test. When I say go, you will run as fast as you can through the obstacles. Okay?"

"Yeah I think so." Nicholas was not scared. He did many obstacle courses at his old school in Murmansk.

"GO!" Shouted Arthro.

Nicholas dodged and darted through the

obstacles like nothing, but they were not what he expected. Instead of ropes, there were razor sharp barbed blades spinning at 100 miles per hour. But Nicholas navigated all the deadly obstacles with ease and got to the end in 28.36 seconds, a record breaker.

When Nicholas got back to the start, he got a clap on the back and a "Congratulations" from Dr. Arthro. Then he was escorted back to his cell. Thirty minutes later an envelope was slipped under his cell door.

It read:

To Nicholas,

You did a superb job in the obstacle course. I am also pleased to inform you that you have been picked as an undercover killer for the Russian Government's spy organization, The Widows. Congratulations, and welcome to the team.

Sincerely, Dr. Arthro

Nicholas could not make heads or tails of it. But he knew people were going to die. For worse or for better, he did not know.

The next day Nicholas was escorted without a bag over his head to a boat. They drove for 15 minutes, and then the man in a black suit stopped at a small sandy island and dumped Nicholas off the boat and sped away.

Nicholas did not have to wait long for another man in a black suit to come and bring him to what was called the training ground. First the retinal scan, then a hill of sand opened up to another secret base. Except this one was teeming with girls and boys. There was no school tour. Just a sign that said undercover killers. Nicholas assumed that was where he was supposed to go. He was correct.

There was a door leading into a classroom filled with very grim-looking kids. The teacher whose name was Mr. Shang told Nicholas to sit and he would catch on quickly. And he did. On that particular day the class was learning about long-term undercover missions and how they would be assigned a mission to kill off the enemy.

Nicholas caught on quickly and soon became top of the class. Meaning, he got first pick on his mission.

He looked through the list of missions. He immediately picked the assassination of Grace Evans, the prime minister of Britain. He picked this mission because just a fortnight ago she took away the U.K.'s trade relations with his home country Russia. He felt compelled to get revenge because he loved Russia and would protect it at all costs.

Ch. 4 - Undercover

Nicholas was on his mission. He was three months in, and he had to stay undercover for one more week. Then he would be able to kill Grace Evans for her betrayal. He had been disguised as a normal schoolboy for three months. To him it felt like weight being lifted off his shoulders. He missed being a schoolboy, but it was short-lived.

The time had come. The kill was going to happen today. All Nicholas had to do was get past the guards at the front door of the prime minister's office, then get in with the lockpicker the Widows gave him and kill Evans!

He was approaching the two young, but very large guards outside of the office. He was dressed just like the guards. The Widows had put stilts on his shoes to make him look taller.

He was now standing in front of the men. Nicholas said, "The boss sent me to replace you." He pointed at the guard on the left. He nodded and walked down the hallway.

Now, all he had to do was tranquilize the other guard. Nicholas was as fast as a bullet! He pulled out the tranq gun and shot him in one slick motion. Then he took out the lock picker and put it in the lock. There was a click, and the door swung open.

Without wasting a moment, Nicholas had a gun pointed at Evans' forehead. She sat defenseless.

"Please let me talk before you kill me," she said

in a surprisingly calm voice.

"Fine!"

What she said was very intriguing. She said, "Do you know why you are here on this mission?"

"Because I want to get revenge. You know what you did."

"I didn't do anything. They did. They made me take away the UK's trade relations with Russia. So they could manipulate you into killing me."

"What? That's impossible."

"Just put down the gun, and I will tell you everything. And we can take down Vladimir Kuznetsov. And the Widows." Nicholas lowered the gun and set it on the ground, but he kept his guard up.

"As I said, you have been manipulated and the man behind all this is not even Vladimir Kuznetsov. It is Malcolm Petrov, the president of Russia."

Ch. 4 - Betrayal and Assassination

The next thing he knew, he was sitting next to whom he had thought was his worst enemy, riding in her limousine. Nicholas and Evans had a table in front of them, and Nicholas was in the middle of drawing a layout of Petrov's estate. They were going to do the unthinkable. They were planning to assassinate Malcolm Petrov!

Nicholas could see that Evans was actually a good person, and he understood, why he had to be the one to kill Petrov.

The time had come. Nicholas was disguised as Evans' son, and they were going to have a meeting with Petrov about the finalization of the U.K.'s decision to stop trade with Russia.

The plan was: Nicholas would come into the estate, and he would ask Petrov where the restroom was. When he was told, he would pretend to go to the toilet, but once out of site of Petrov, he would sneak into the palace and wait until the meeting was over. Then when Petrov was walking Evans to the door, he would go up to the top of the main stairwell and snipe Petrov from above. Then he'd jump out the rear window and meet Evans at the limousine and seem shocked at what had happened.

Nicholas had been given one pistol with one bullet. He only had one chance. They got out of the limousine to find Petrov waiting for them with a large fake smile. The plan was a go.

"Welcome to my estate."

"Thank you. Could you please direct me to the restroom?" said Nicholas.

"Of course, this way," Petrov exclaimed, pointing in the direction of the palace. "Up the stairs and to the left," said Petrov.

Nicholas ran up the steps and positioned himself. Now all he had to do was wait. Then suddenly, he heard a scream. He recognized it immediately as Evans'.

He ran down the stairs following the source of the screaming. He ran into what seemed to be a living room to find Petrov pinning Evans against the wall by the throat. Nicholas knew immediately that Petrov was on to them. Petrov did not realize that he had a visitor. So Nicholas knew he had the advantage. And he took it. He took out the pistol, aimed and shot. Suddenly, Petrov sagged and sank to the floor, groaning in pain.

He was dying, and Nicholas knew he could not give chase, so he grabbed Evans' arm and ran out to the limousine and told the chauffeur to get out of there. When they were out of the estate, Evans was still gasping for air. But she managed to say, "Oh, thank God," and "Thank you, Nicholas," before she fell asleep.

Nicholas heard barking. He looked back, and a large pack of vicious looking guard dogs were chasing them. One ran up alongside the car and rammed it so hard, it caved in. The chauffeur punched the gas, and they sped off, leaving the dogs behind.

Ch 5 - Return

When he got back, Nicholas sank into a chair in Evans' office and said, "Before you ask, no, I do not want to join a little team of yours. I think I just want to be a normal school boy, but maybe not in Russia."

Then he fell asleep, and when he woke up, he was on a park bench at a trolley stop where he must have been dropped off. And he was happy. Happy that he would never be a spy again and happy that he was now normal. But he would never forget what had happened those last few months.

He realized he had no home to go back to, now that his father was gone, but like any good spy, he had a plan B. He got on the trolley, rode to the airport and caught a plane to the US. He decided to start a new life, living in peace, off the grid somewhere where no one would find him.

ABOUT THE AUTHOR *Hi, my name is Ella Meltzer. I am 11 years old, and I go to Summit Middle School. I am in the sixth grade, and I love to read and write. I also love to play sports like soccer, and I am on a swim team. I love animals. I have two dogs - one is fully grown, and the other is only 10 months old. I love to travel and learn new things.*

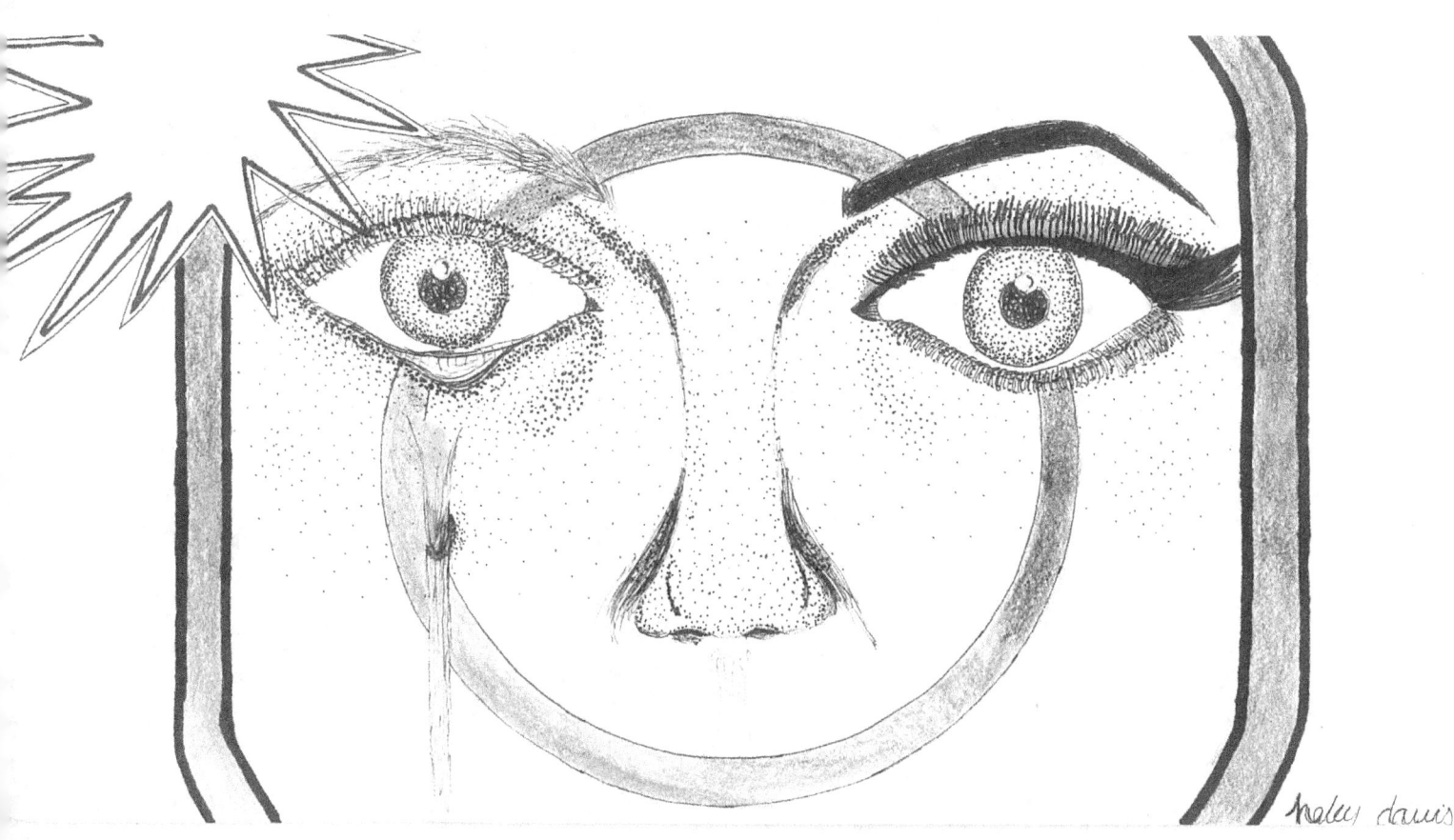

Instagram Eyes
Mixed Media | Haley Davis, Grade 11

My name is Haley Davis. I am 17 years old, and I have lived in Breckenridge, Colorado my entire life. I am a junior at Summit High School. I chose this medium because I love taking pictures. I create art with nature, food and things I find beautiful as my subject matter. I love making art because it gives me a way to express myself. My art also allows others to have their own interpretation.

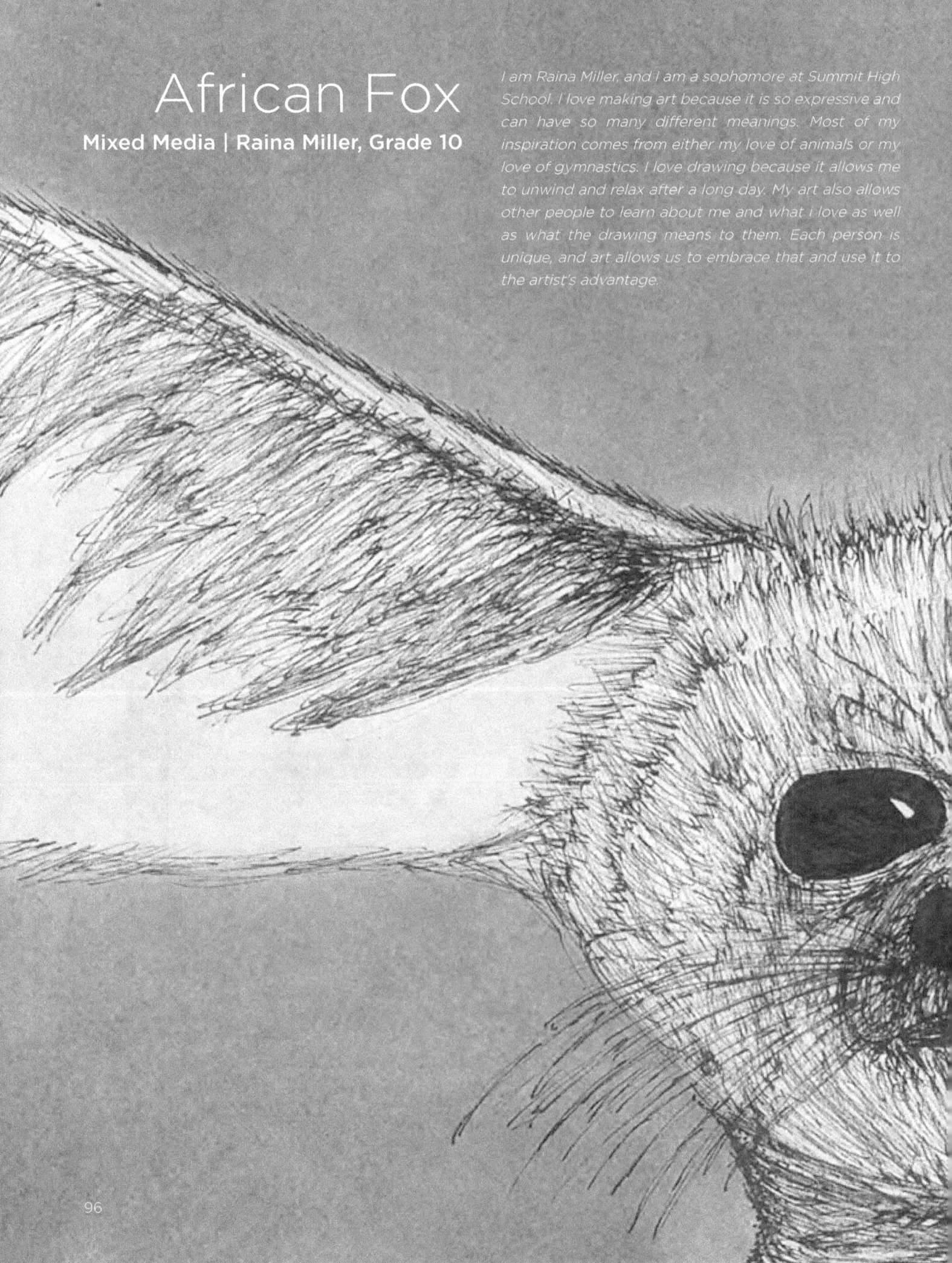

African Fox
Mixed Media | Raina Miller, Grade 10

I am Raina Miller, and I am a sophomore at Summit High School. I love making art because it is so expressive and can have so many different meanings. Most of my inspiration comes from either my love of animals or my love of gymnastics. I love drawing because it allows me to unwind and relax after a long day. My art also allows other people to learn about me and what i love as well as what the drawing means to them. Each person is unique, and art allows us to embrace that and use it to the artist's advantage.

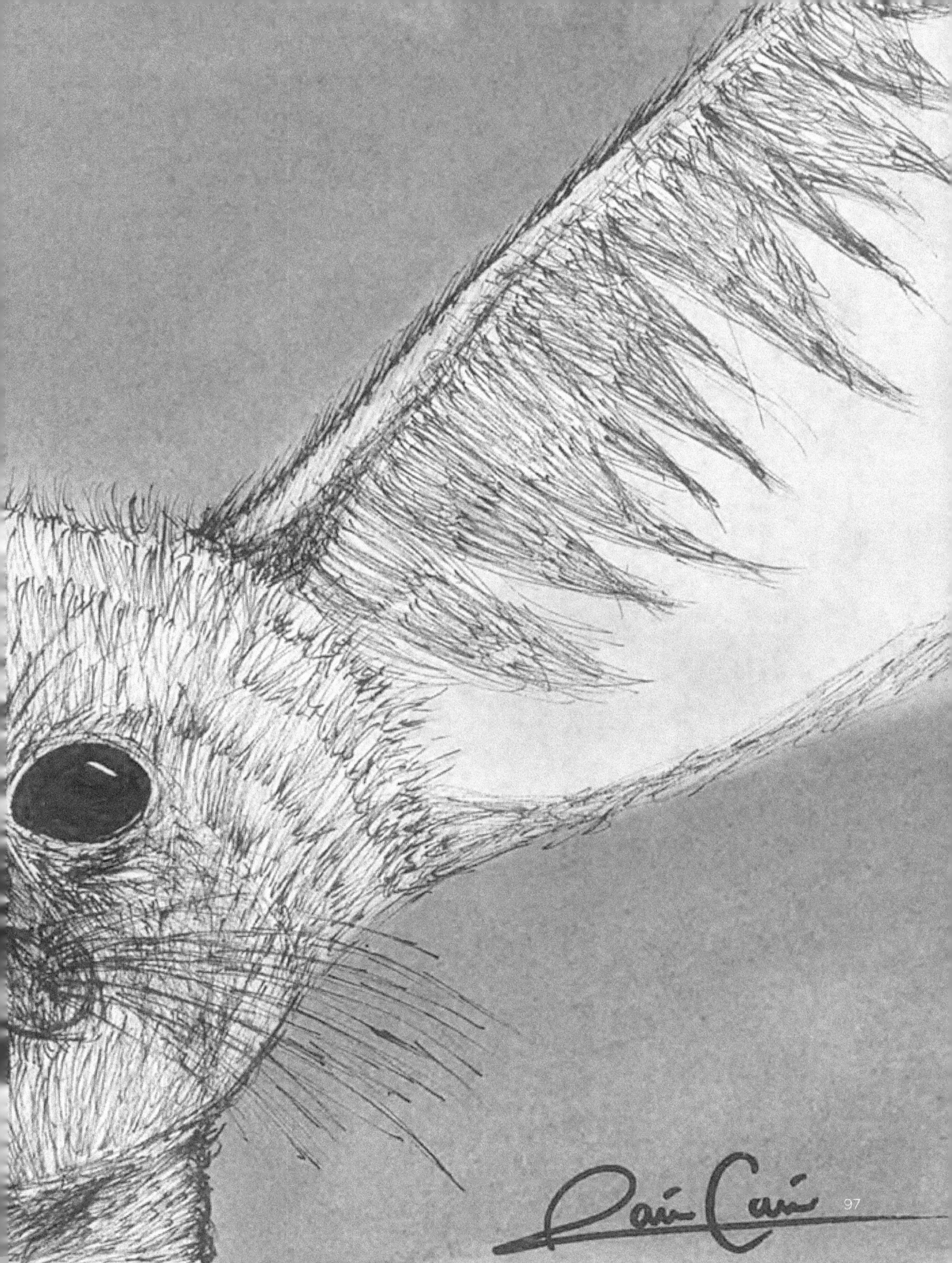

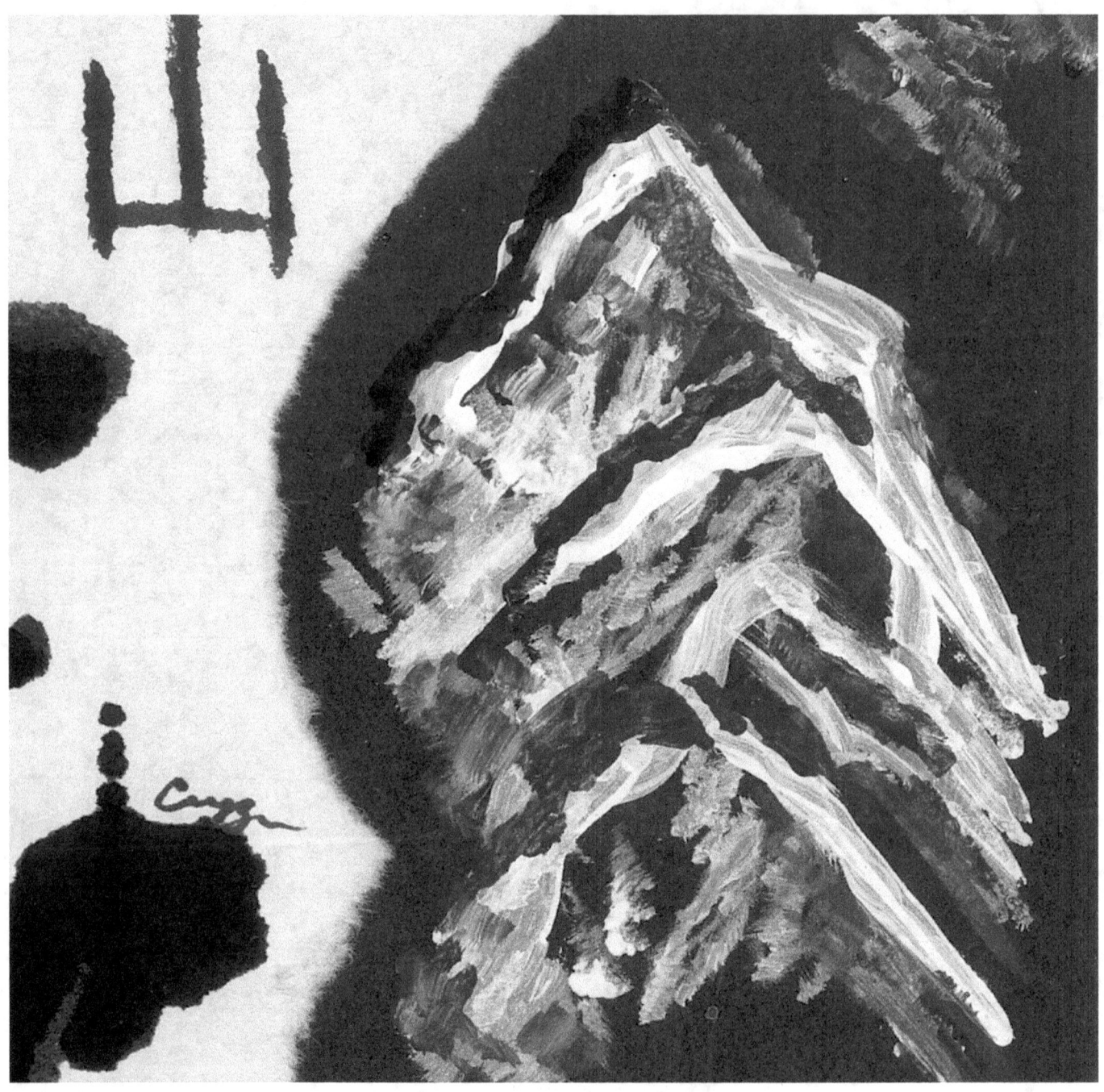

Untitled

Mixed Media | Chase Byers, Grade 11

Born and raised in the vast mountains of Colorado, Chase Byers continues to pioneer in his own artistic discoveries. Studying through the International Baccalaureate program Chase has been able to experience success, failure, studio time, and workshops. Starting his professional career in 2017 alongside Summit High School and BreckCreate, Chase has focused on producing beautiful pieces using primarily charcoal and photography. By revealing cultural elements and reflections of master painters, Chase has been passionate about creating art that teaches and expresses a message, whether it is placed on the street or in premier galleries, and therefore never fails to impress.

Hard Work
By Cole Stuckey

I slammed my fist into the wall with a fresh wave of tears pouring down my face. My fist stung, but I ignored it, too distraught to care about anything at the moment.

As I walked into the locker room, everyone had the same face on. We just lost to our rival, and it was all over. Each of my gloves was on the opposite side of the room in a matter of seconds, and my helmet was thrown down on top of my bag until it rolled away and stopped near the trash can. Sticks were strewn around the locker room, along with other gloves and a few helmets that were probably thrown down in anger. There were many sobs echoing around the room, seemingly bouncing right back and spreading the sadness like a dark, gloomy cloud.

Coach came in, and he didn't seem as disappointed as we all expected.

"Guys, that was the hardest game I have ever seen you play," he said interrupting the silence, excepting a few sobbs here and there. "You left everything out there, and that's the only thing we wanted you to do."

Our second Coach walked in, Coach Wren, and he also had a similar face on.

"Boys, we had a great year, and you should be proud of it. They just out-played us."

To our surprise Coach kept talking, "I'm gonna let you on a secret here." He paused for a second. "Everyone kept saying at the beginning of the season, 'Your hands are full, Wren. Oh, you've got some kids in that group.' Everyone doubted what this team could do, and I was ready to prove them wrong. And that's exactly what we did. No one thought we could win a game and make it anywhere in playoffs. But look at where we're sitting right now. We played the toughest came against the #1 team that anyone ever has."

By now everyone could feel the passion throughout the room, and in Coach's words as he spoke.

"Let's get out of here with our heads held high, and I want everyone to be proud of what they did this season."

All three of the coaches surprisingly stayed in the locker room as everyone started to get dressed and the mood started to lift. Jokes started to float around the room and goodbyes came along with it. Once everyone was undressed, we decided to walk out as a team, this being our last time together for the season, save a few stick and pucks here and there.

Since that day, I now know that someone is going to be better, or faster, and stronger than you, and that you can never stop working and pushing to the next level. Even though my team might have lost, we are still proud of the work we accomplished.

ABOUT THE AUTHOR *My name is Cole Stuckey, and I live in Breckenridge, Colorado. I love to play hockey in the winter and dirt bike in the summer.*

Still Life
Graphite and Colored Pencil | Kiara Gelbman, Grade 10

My name is Kiara Gelbman. I am currently a student at Summit High School in Colorado, but I am originally from New York. I love drawing because it gives me the ability to let my creativity flow. My art changes the way I view the world around me. In my work, I capture real objects and put them on paper. I also love to abstract real objects and make them my own. Some of my favorite techniques include using pencil to create a black and white value as well as adding accents of color.

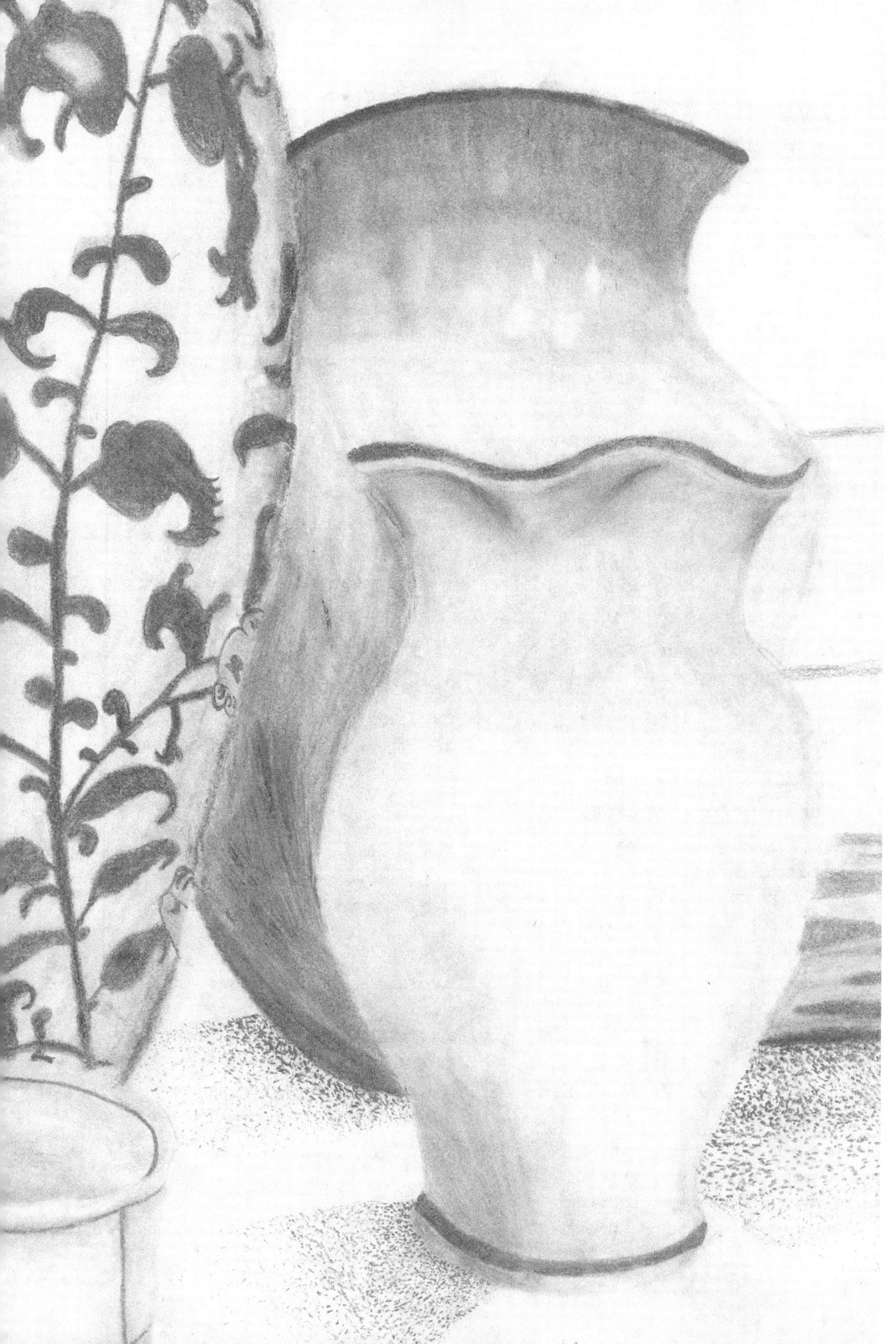

Growth and Strength
by Luci Brady

Strength and growth come only through continuous effort and struggle.
-Napoleon Hill

Independence and strength - something you should NEVER grow up without, but I had to learn them somehow.

As everyone knows, (especially parents) when kids come home from school, they put their lunchbox on the counter and plan to empty it later. But then...somehow, their parents usually end up doing it for them. Or when they are getting ready for bed, their parents say, "Johnny! Clean up your Toy Story, Star Wars mega playhouse set before you get to bed!"

But then they wake up in the morning, "Hey Johnny, I cleaned up your Toy Story, Star Wars mega playhouse set for you last night," and they respond, "Eh, thanks." That's the normal routine for kids and parents.

And we kids should be grateful for that, and most of us are, but we get a little distracted.

Soon enough, (hopefully) we will learn independence, and doing this for ourselves will come naturally. Our parents do a lot for us, but with one little flip of the switch, everything can change.

And this is how I learned...from the strongest, bravest, most extraordinary mother.

Who currently has stage 4 stomach cancer. With three crazy kids. Me, my middle sister who is 11, and my youngest sister who is 8. Plus a dog and a husband.

As you can imagine, it was really hard at first because I didn't even really understand how bad it was. And I still don't. Most of the time, it feels like any other regular day. But then not.

Sometimes, I get home from school, and three hours later my parents come home, rushing up to the room. Concerns, crying, appointments for every kind of doctor you can think of. The hole, where your mother would be, making your breakfast, hugging you goodbye as you go to school.

As a child I knew of the general idea of cancer: bad, scary, painful, deadly. But I never would ever think that it would happen to my family! It's scary knowing that my mom could die. I don't really understand.

I mean I have heard many friends say that their grandparents have cancer. And that is sad for sure, but it is different when it is your mother.

Life has changed in many ways. It's more complicated now. My mother can't do her job, so my dad has to do two full time jobs. That leads to a bunch of, well, let's just get to the point: a messy house, sisters crying and screaming, an 11 year old sassy sister, and an 8 year old who acts like a 6 or 5 year old.

And who is going to fix that? I mean, we used to have people come every other week to clean our house and do the laundry. But with a shedding hair dog, messy kids and a big house, let's be honest, it's going to need a lot more cleaning! I try to help out as much as I can, you know, doing the dishes, cleaning the house. But it does not always end up that way. I mean, I am a kid, just a kid. Writing this right now makes me realize even more how I should be helping out more.

Honestly, most of the time, kids to go for their mother for everything.

"Mama, can you help me!?"

"Mama, Mama she is being mean!"

"Mama! Where are you!?"

As funny as that sounds, it was also very frustrating because when my dad was doing one of the two full time jobs, it was just me, my sisters and my mom. My mom just can't do all those things for us any more because she needs to rest and heal. My dad cares about my mom very much. He always tells us, I mean ALWAYS tells us not to fight or cause stress because stress makes mama's cancer worse.

While mama is at chemo or sleeping and daddy is at work, me and my sisters end up with a lot of time alone, at the house. We are not allowed to leave the house, so we get bored, staying at home, watching TV. And we want to go and do something, but sometimes we can't. We kids, we want to just go, go, go! We want to be with our friends, go bike riding, watch a movie. Luckily, we have so many friends that will come and bring us somewhere to go do something, so it is not always that terrible.

There are a lot of things, though, that get changed. Different people come pick us up from our activities, or we end of having to stay home alone sometimes doing nothing. So, what do we do? My parents don't have time to be involved with everything that happens at school.

So, I am left to do it myself. Most of my friends tell me, "If I don't get in the Gold Honor roll, I can't ski any more,"

"If I get three 3.5, I will get a NEW bike!"

But with me, there are no expectations, my parents don't care that much if I get three 2's! But that is a problem because I am a very organized person, with my schedule and everything. I can't stand not doing well! So I end up setting my own expectations. A lot of people say I am an overachiever. I just keep doing what I am doing.

Throughout this struggle of my Dad, my sisters, me, and...my Mom, I know we have all grown stronger.

After all, "Strength and growth come only through continuous effort and struggle."

ABOUT THE AUTHOR *I am Luci Brady, and I love the mountains. When it comes to skiing to hiking, I am in the mountains. I also love to write poetry and write stories. There have been a lot of ups and downs this year, but I know my family will always be at my side.*

Sushi Delight

**Ceramic
Abraham Lopez, Grade 6**

Hi, my name is Abraham Lopez, and I'm from Denver CO. I have been living in Summit County for my whole life, from when I was a few months old to 11 years old. One of my hobbies is art. I have been making art for a long time.

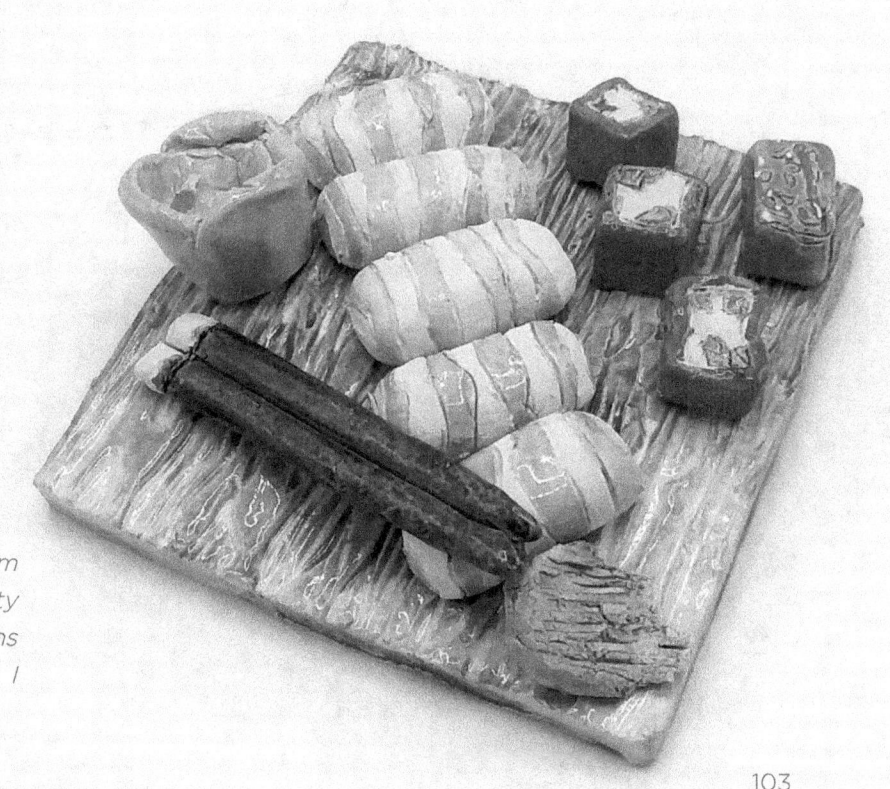

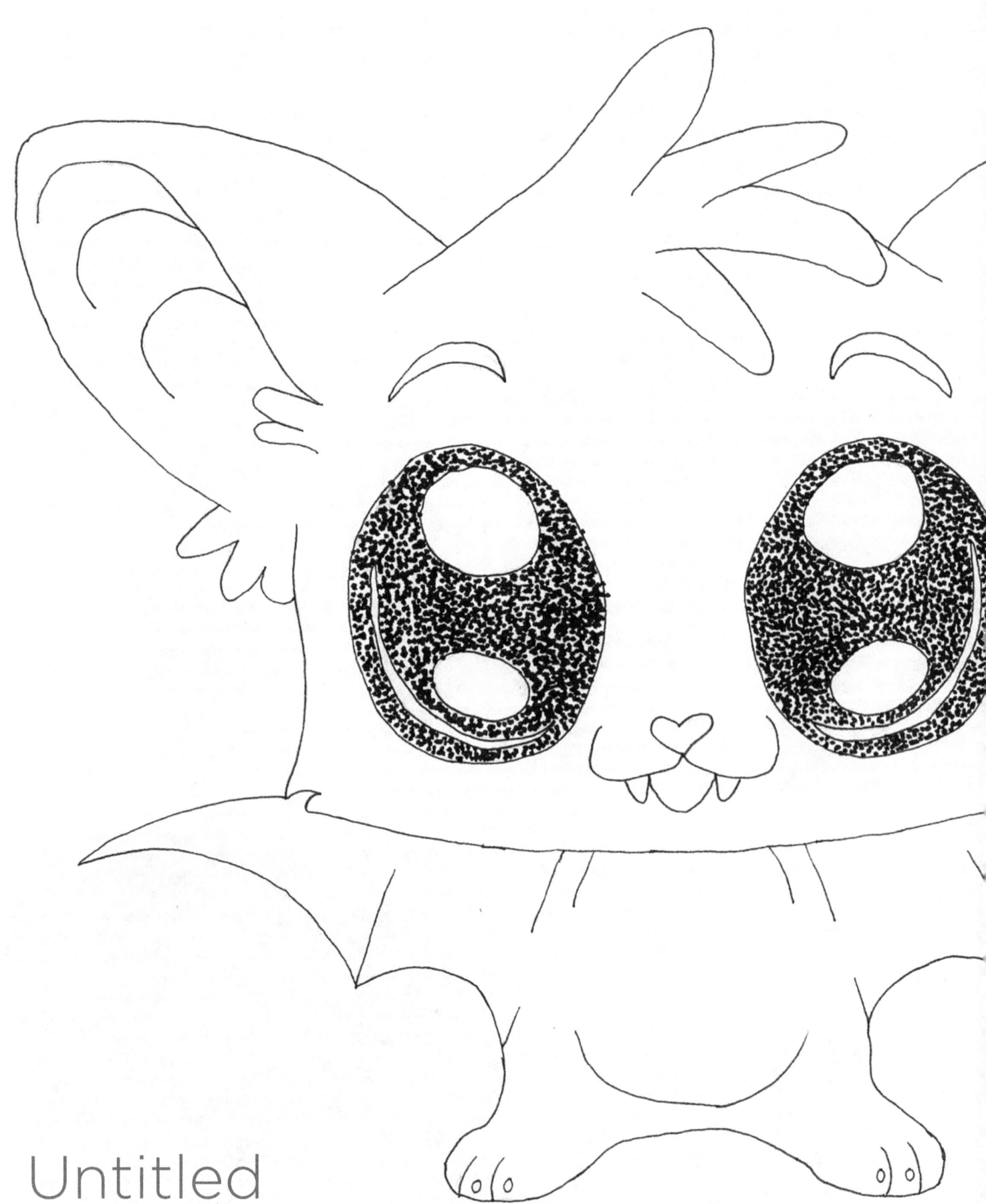

Untitled

Pen/Ink | Jennifer Amador, Grade 11

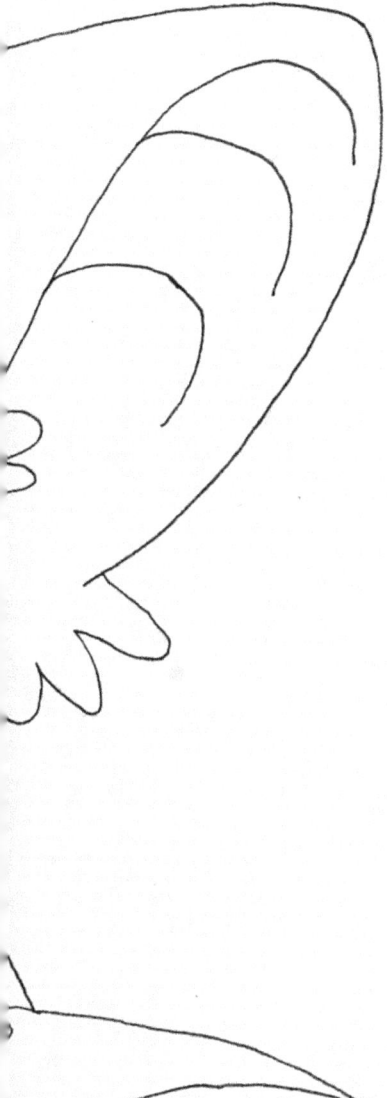

Acknowledgments

We'd like to first thank all of the supporters of Breckenridge Creative Arts and the arts in Summit County. We are lucky to have so many opportunities to experience great exhibits, classes, and art-related events.

Thank you, also, to all the writers and artists who submitted their work for this book. You are amazing! Thanks for being brave enough to put yourself out there and share your creativity with us. We know it's not always easy. We wish we could have included all of your submissions, but we look forward to future volumes where we can keep highlighting our local talent.

Thank you to all the teachers and BCA staff who made this possible, especially Karen Fisher, High School Art Teacher and art instructor at Breckenridge Creative Arts, Andria Barberi, 6th grade New Voices in Literature teacher, Andrea Stark, 8th grade Language Arts teacher, Harriet Hoffman, Middle School Art Teacher, and Sarah Revel, High School Art Teacher.

A special thanks to our bookstore partner, Next Page Books & Nosh, for their generous support of this project.

And a special thank you to all who purchased this collection. Your donations will go to support a favorite local organization benefiting our Summit County Youth, Mountain Mentors.

Graphic Design: Angela Knightley

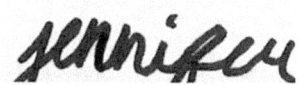

About Breckenridge Creative Arts

Established in 2014, Breckenridge Creative Arts (BCA)—or BreckCreate for short—was developed by the Town of Breckenridge to support and promote arts, culture and creative experiences throughout Breckenridge. This multidisciplinary nonprofit organization is responsible for the successful management of a series of programs, properties and partnerships that collectively animate and populate a cultural corridor in the heart of downtown Breckenridge. From quality performing and visual arts to the development of one of the region's newest arts districts, Breckenridge Creative Arts is a transformative force for Breckenridge and the greater Summit County community.

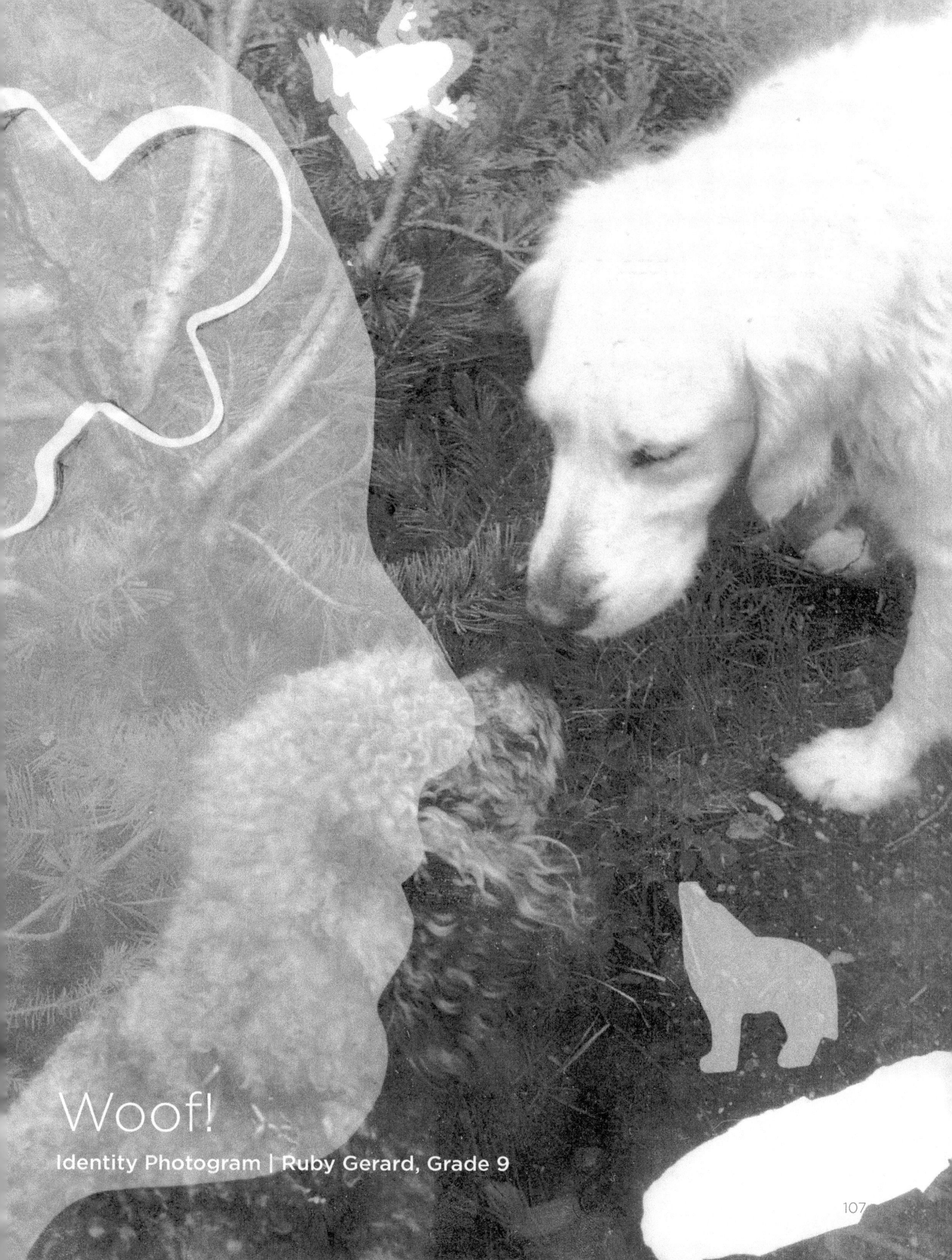

Woof!

Identity Photogram | Ruby Gerard, Grade 9

Dragon
Graphite | William O'Brien, Grade 12

William O'Brien is a current senior at Summit County High School. Art has been a passion of his for as long as he can remember. He plans to attend Western State University in the fall and pursue a Bachelors degree in visual arts.

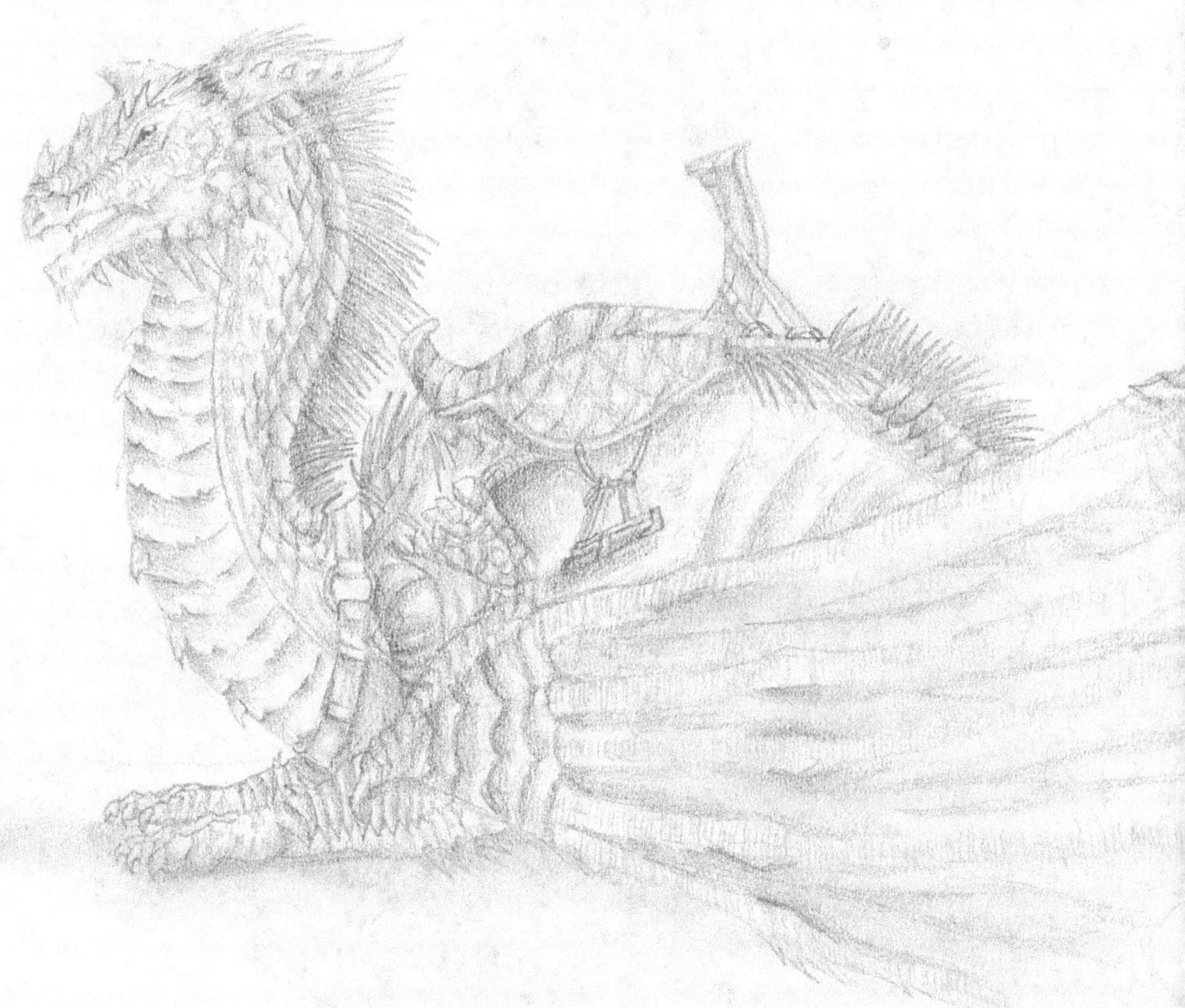

About the After School Writing Club

The After School Writing Club is for middle-school students and meets every Thursday from 5-6:30 pm in Old Masonic Hall. Join us for inspiration, fun, and guidance in creative writing. Each week, the group will tackle new elements of the short story, including character development, plot twists, and creative endings. Students will also have the opportunity to submit work to be featured in a collection of local writing, published annually. To ensure a spot, register online. Walk-ins also welcome, first-come, first-served.

For more information contact sonya@sonyadalrymple.com

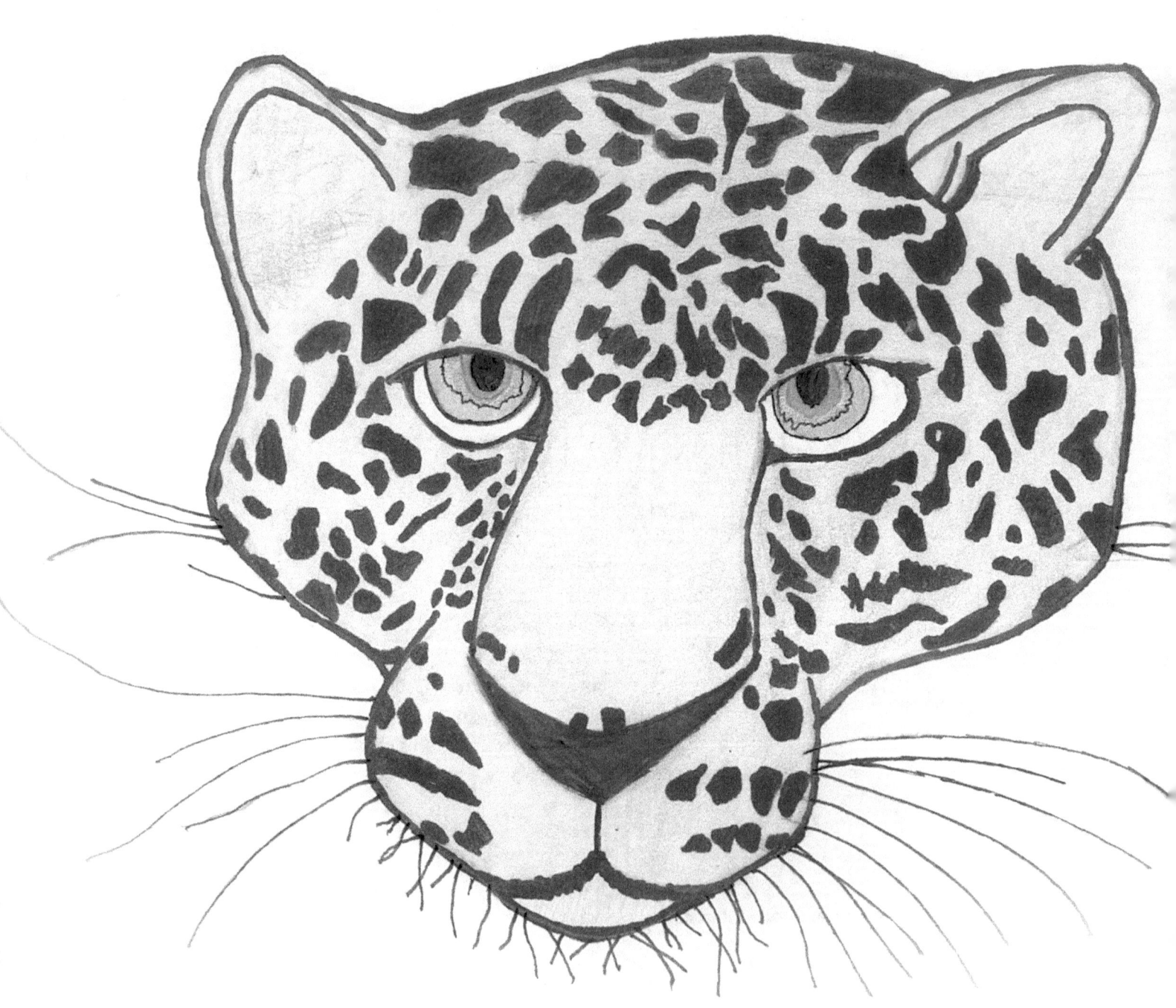

Leopard

Mixed Media | Christopher Lopez, Grade 10